A DAMN NEAR PERFECT GAME

JOE KELLY
with Rob Bradford

A DAMN NEAR PERFECT GAME

Reclaiming America's Pastime

DIVERSION
BOOKS

NEW YORK

For more information, email info@diversionbooks.com

Diversion Books
A division of Diversion Publishing Corp.
www.diversionbooks.com

First Diversion Books edition, March 2023
Hardcover ISBN: 9781635768893
eBook ISBN: 9781635769661

Printed in The United States of America
10 9 8 7 6 5 4 3 2 1

To you, the reader

CONTENTS

A DAMN NEAR PERFECT GAME

THE POWER OF A POUT

By the time our Dodgers' bus pulled up to Minute Maid Park for that late July series in 2020, we already hated the Astros. At least my teammates did, and that was good enough for me. Why? Well, if you watched another team cheat their way to a world championship at your expense, you might have some hard feelings as well.

Heading into that 2020 season, it came to light that the Astros had been brazenly breaking the rules, using a video feed to steal signs and then banging a trash can just behind the dugout to relay what pitches were coming. When I was pitching for the Red Sox as all this was going on in the 2017 season, everybody knew clubs were swiping signs with runners on second base—and even without runners on second, thanks to well-placed video equipment. But the Astros were taking it to another level, and they were doing so on the road to beating the Dodgers in the '17 World Series.

What the Astros were doing wasn't in the same solar system as the rest of baseball.

This trip to Houston was the first time my guys were getting a chance to go face-to-face with the cheaters. And there was more to be pissed about than just the 2017 robbery . The Astros' attitude, once they were caught, was bullshit. All offseason and into spring training that year, they were crying about this and that, showing barely any remorse. They had thrown a lot of their own people under the bus—former coach Alex Cora, former manager A. J. Hinch, former general manager Jeff Luhnow, and former teammate Carlos Beltran—riding the security of the immunity given to the Astros by Major League Baseball. What a joke!

And to top it all off, Astros shortstop Carlos Correa—one of the centerpiece players of that team—was the whiniest of them all. Through an interview with Ken Rosenthal of *The Athletic*, Correa told our guy, Cody Bellinger, "If you don't know the facts, then you've got to shut the fuck up."

For us, that was the last straw. In our clubhouse, 99 percent had a strong desire to kick their ass. It wasn't like we talked about it on a daily basis leading into the teams' reunion. That's not really how baseball players operate, sitting around and sharing feelings. But it was mostly understood.

The Astros hadn't been punished. The team should have been taken away from its owner, Jim Crane. The players should have been hit with the kind of pain afforded Cora and Hinch, who were both forced to sit out of baseball for a year. There should have been a daily peppering of animosity from fans, which wasn't even an option because of the COVID-induced empty ballparks. In our eyes, they had to get some comeuppance. It was coming, although in a form nobody expected—my pouty face.

. . .

You know what the most powerful emotion is? Embarrassment. That's what I gave Carlos Correa. That was his and the Astros' punishment.

Embarrassment is way worse than sadness. You aren't alone in a room. You can't keep it to yourself. It's there for everyone to see. I know. I have had my fair share, both on and off the baseball field. The most common occurrences come after simple baseball-playing failure. I have the ability to throw a baseball like few in the world, yet there are times when I allow the opposition to get the better of me, immediately engulfing me in the shame of letting my teammates down. It's the worst.

The impact of the emotion is made more potent due to its unpredictability. Baseball is life, and life is baseball. And embarrassment is part of it all.

My dad, Joe Kelly Sr., taught me so much and meant the world to me—with his on-field embraces after each of my two World Series championships truly punctuating those paths. But the lessons weren't always easy ones, including understanding the power that comes with the most potent of all emotions. My old man used to be at the center of a lot of embarrassment for me, but more about that later. It's complicated.

Now it was the son of Joseph Kelly Sr. who stood to embarrass the former first overall pick—the superstar who showed no remorse for his and his team's transgressions.

Before I took the mound that day, I was pissed. Afterward, I was pissed. But while actually pitching in the sixth inning—with the Dodgers comfortably leading the Astros by three runs—not so much. It's a state of mind I have always been fascinated by. Why, with all those people watching and so much at stake, don't I let my mind wander into a million different places? I love psychology. Love it. Majored in it. And when it comes to baseball, the sport is a treasure trove for this fascination.

I can understand where Hall of Famer Yogi Berra was coming from when he said: "Baseball is 90 percent mental. The other half is physical." The point is this: There is a lot going on when you get put on center stage on a baseball field.

In this case, the sense of normalcy wasn't really from the act of throwing the baseball. I threw eighteen pitches that day—fastballs, curveballs, changeups. Some found their way to the spot I intended; others didn't. What really felt right was all the jibber-jabber in between each offering. I'd had plenty of that in my past. The whiny Astros were bringing me back to my roots, surfacing the kind of awareness that is often found in all baseball players' initial introduction to the game. Competition plus animosity plus grudges can often lead to the most memorable moments on a baseball diamond. Here was proof.

After a first-pitch pop-up by José Altuve, I faced Alex Bregman. Fastball. Curveball. Curveball. All outside the strike zone. Then came one more heater, one that got away more than the others and sailed up over Bregman's head. Ball four. Take your base. Let the chirping from the whiners begin.

Because all those Astros thought I had purposely thrown at Bregman, they suddenly started yelling my way. In my mind, these were the entitled rich kids who were so used to believing their shit don't stink they thought it was their God-given right to tell the poor kids what was what. They were the spoiled kids from the movie *The Sandlot* who never had to face the music, thinking, *Sure, we cheated, but so what? We don't have to be accountable to the media. Everyone should leave us alone.*

Sorry, that's not how this works.

The blueprint for this wasn't unfamiliar. I immediately thought back to some rich, travel ball team kids we ran into in Las Vegas as eleven-year-olds (travel ball is a form of youth baseball played outside a team's immediate area). They thought they could talk trash to us while we were playing Ping-Pong during our off time. That led to what was technically my first baseball-induced fight. But the voice that rang through my head was that of a guy named Rich Krzysiak—one of my first coaches and still one of my favorites.

"Tough nuts, kick butts!"

This was Rich's rallying cry. In other words, even though you barely have hair under your armpits, take no shit from anybody. The attitude and intent permeated my psyche and lived there for what had been twenty years. It manifested itself during an AAU (Amateur Athletic Union) game in Palm Springs, when some well-to-do kids on the other team started yelling at me, leading to me storming into our dugout and exclaiming: "You hear those kids! You think they can rattle me?" Rich loved that. I loved that Rich loved it. And now we were all going to get another reminder of that mentality.

My first reaction to the Astros was simply to yawn. (Lesson: Facial expressions can really rile major leaguers.)

Then, after I almost hit Bregman with a few pickoff throws, Michael Brantley pounded a curveball into the turf, allowing our first baseman, Max Muncy, to throw to shortstop Corey Seager, who threw back to me at first base for the attempted inning-ending double play. Immediately after Brantley safely crossed the bag, that's when I heard Houston's seventy-one-year-old manager, Dusty Baker.

"Just get on the mound, little fucker!"

That, along with Brantley narrowly missing the back of my leg with his cleat, started getting my blood pumping. *Here we go.* I so desperately wanted to echo my words back in Palm Springs: "They thought they could rattle me!"

Now comes the fun part.

With the Astros still all hot and bothered, I walked the next batter, Yuli Gurriel. That brought up Correa. The pain I was about to inflict on this guy had nothing to do with baseball seams between a couple of ribs. It was about supplying him—and his teammates—with the ultimate pain, the kind that comes with embarrassment.

I knew he could hit fastballs, and I couldn't locate mine that day anyway, so that was never an option. Instead, I started him off with a changeup, which I also had no feel for, as was evident by the ball flying up over his head. That pitch elicited a new layer of crying from the Astros' dugout and a tough-guy look from Correa. While we were clearly in this cauldron of baseball-playing venom, one thing struck me after that first pitch to Correa: How stupid were they? For guys who had played baseball all their lives, you'd think they would understand that if I really wanted to hit him, it would be courtesy of 99 mph in his side, not an off-speed offering. *Whatever.*

Five straight curveballs. That's what I finished off Correa with, culminating in an inning-ending swing and a miss. I knew he couldn't hit that pitch, so that's what I threw. It wasn't all that complicated.

Cue the embarrassment for Carlos.

As if Coach Krzysiak were waiting for me in the dugout, I reacted, "Nice swing, bitch!" Correa, the player who had shown no remorse for his cheating, had entered into an emotion he likely wasn't all that familiar with. He was humbled, and he didn't like it. Baseball can offer so many powerful lessons, with this potentially serving as one of them. Correa wasn't being a good student.

So, about the pout . . .

When Correa started staring back at me while I was walking toward the dugout, my thoughts were straightforward: He was being a baby. He was being a brat. So, at the end of the day, this wasn't about memes or television broadcasts or what might happen. This was the definitive way I politely wanted to get the message to Mr. Correa that he was being infantile. Admittedly, I had no previous experience relaying such a message on a baseball field, and that was because I hadn't come across a group quite so whiny. Not Little League. Not high school. Not college. Not the minors. Certainly not in the big leagues. I had no experience with such a situation.

And that was an example of what should be part of the beauty of this game. What you see is what you should get. Raw emotion should be part of the solution to baseball's current issues, not the problem. In this case, such a thing was delivered to Correa via the only pout of my entire life that wasn't directed at someone four years old or younger.

Bottom lip jutted out. Eyes squinting. Face scrunched up. The *Oxford English Dictionary* describes it as "pushing one's lips or one's bottom lip forward as an expression of petulant annoyance." Yup.

Now we were in it. This was the pampered AAU kid across the Ping-Pong table in Las Vegas from twenty years before.

I kept going. "Hey, that shit is easy. Fucking easy!"

Finally, Correa responded. "Throw your fastball, bitch."

"Oh, yeah. I'll throw my fastball right down the middle for you. Shut the fuck up," I said, firmly believing what was done was done.

I think it started hitting home for Carlos. Embarrassment has different stages, after all. There is the immediate sense of shock. Then there are the emotional daggers that start to set in. And finally comes the usually fruitless attempt to rectify the situation. "You struck me out, so what?" he started yelling. What? That was his response? The Astros came on the field and so did our guys, and that was that. No punches. No pushing. Everyone knew that in the heart of the COVID chaos at that time, physical altercations would result in triple the punishment from Major League Baseball, so the back-and-forth verbiage would have to suffice.

What was done was done. Or so I thought.

CHAPTER ONE

THE EMBRACE OF BASEBALL

Wake up!

Put down your phone. Pause those video games. Stop looking at your smartwatch.

Baseball is waiting for you.

I'm talking to the fans. I'm talking to the kids. I'm talking to the parents. I'm talking to those who gave up on the game, or those who never took the time to introduce themselves to it in the first place. I'm talking to the players. I'm talking to the coaches. I'm talking to the owners. I'm talking to the commissioner.

Consider these words to be freezing cold water splashed on your face. Jump up and soak it all in. It's unfortunate that we have gotten to this point where such an awakening is necessary, but so be it. Here you go. This is a straight ball right down the middle. Baseball is a gift; now it's time to unwrap it.

There aren't a lot of things in life that can impact every nook and cranny of your existence like baseball. That's a fact. Relationships. Upbringing. Entertainment. Amazement. Conversations. And, of course, a tidal wave of life lessons. It's all right there. That's what baseball offers. Did you forget?

I haven't.

Understand that I'm not here to suggest that my path to this point—as a major league relief pitcher who never made an All-Star team (yet)—is so special that it should be separated from the rest of the baseball-playing world. I simply have been living this life inside the sport, looking all around, and not always liking what I see. Sure, I have a story, as does everyone else touched by this game. But I want to make sure we don't forget about how baseball has the power to shape lives, like it did with me. And, more important, that we keep that conversation going.

I'm lucky. I'm reminded of the mission every single day. Every. Single. Day. We should all be so fortunate. And we can be.

For me, it's not just the uniform, the paycheck, the opportunity to throw a baseball in front of thousands of fans, or the thrill and agony that come with actually competing at the highest level of the sport. Sure, that's all part of it. But the real important stuff that baseball has cloaked me in has come courtesy of my everyday existence. It shapes lives, brings out emotions, and, maybe above all, actually makes you think. Big-league ballplayer or not, that's what baseball can do to you.

Do you want an example? How about the power of a simple pout?

The impact of this game sneaks up on you all the time. Sometimes it's the flames of emotion that come with a great pitch, a bat flip, or success in just the right moment. When I walked off the mound after striking out a third straight batter in the final game of the 2018 World Series, I knew what was going on. I had just pumped 99 mph past Cody Bellinger, and we were three outs from the end game, living life as the world champions of baseball.

"Fuck, yeah!"

Those two words? They jumped out of my body. And I'm not sorry they did.

My heart rate skyrocketed, popping the veins in my neck. There was also the sight of a dugout full of teammates experiencing the same joy. All of it was the punctuation of five seconds of life-altering emotion. This is what baseball can do. And, believe me, you know when it is happening. It's the kind of instant gratification that human beings crave these days more than ever, and—despite what some sports fans say—it's what baseball offers over and over again.

Those shock-to-the-system moments are there time and again. Little League. High school. College. Pros. You name it.

But what separates this game from all the others is that with the infinite outcomes of each pitch and each swing, these moments in baseball catch you by surprise. For me, my reminder is seventeen feet tall and engulfs an entire wall outside a barbershop in Silver Lake, California. That's where a simple pout says so much.

Not everybody gets to have a guttural reaction to a baseball-induced flare of emotion immortalized by a talented artist. I'm one of the fortunate ones in this respect. The creator of the mural, Jonas Never, and the image's host, Floyd's 99 Barbershop, afforded me that, putting paint to the wall just about a month after I pointed my bottom lip in the direction of Carlos Correa, back on Labor Day weekend in 2020.

I'm not going to lie. Such a thing is a pretty big deal. Being on baseball cards and brick walls will never get old. And, let's be honest, for baseball as a whole, you aren't going to find a better weapon to strip away the idea that the game is devoid of emotion and anticipation than what that portrait delivers.

Still, what the artistry should truly bring to the surface is a reminder—a reminder that so much of baseball is life, with all the highs, lows, and unplanned manifestations of memories sometimes unwittingly put on display. In my case, all of it was a product of this one, simple facial expression.

I can throw a ball 100 mph, dunk a basketball, and still jump a skateboard over a sofa. But who knew my mentalis—you know them as your chin muscles—would allow for such a powerful snapshot when it comes to another meaningful athletic achievement. Thanks again, baseball!

The pouty-face moment wasn't all that complicated. A lot of such moments aren't. Take, for instance, when a player steals a base, hits a home run, or pumps triple-digits past a hitter. What you see is what you get. But this is also the beauty of baseball. There are always layers upon layers upon layers to the story before, during, and certainly after. Me taunting Correa with my bottom lip was no exception.

• • •

I didn't think much of the moment in Houston throughout the following days. But the business of baseball wouldn't allow for a complete disconnect from the Houston back-and-forth, thanks to another random round of punishment—my suspension, which was originally eight games. (Eight games! Twenty months later, Josh Donaldson makes racial insinuations to my White Sox teammate Tim Anderson, and he gets a one-game suspension. I make a funny face. Eight games.)

And just when I thought MLB had stepped aside, and we had all moved on from the punishment portion of the process, it resurfaced more than two months later. Sometimes baseball just can't get out of its own way when it comes to this stuff, as my wife (of all people) and I found out.

Smack dab in the middle of October 2020, with the Dodgers and Astros on the verge of meeting again in the World Series, MLB got in touch with Ashley. Because of the COVID-induced postseason bubble in Texas, both the National League and American League champs would be staying in the same hotel, which of course meant the strong possibility of bumping into some of the guys from Houston, including Correa. They wanted Ashley to convince me to meet up with Carlos and agree with him that we wouldn't fight. And to top things off, MLB would have security escort me everywhere in this Lone Star State COVID bubble to make sure I didn't get into it with him off the field.

Ashley just laughed. Neither of us could believe it. Her response: "Good luck with that. I'm not going to tell him that. Joe's crazy. The only way you're going to stop him is by making the Astros lose and go away."

I was furious. I told Ashley if the Astros found themselves facing us in the World Series, and we ended up in the same hotel with those guys, she should put our kids—Knox and the twins—down so I could go wait for the Astros. Just me. No teammates. If they didn't want that to happen, then they could either make sure Houston lost or pay the money to be in different hotels. Otherwise, there was going to be a big problem.

So, they wanted me to quarantine as though I were in a prison, escorted by security everywhere—basically handcuffing me to the table at dinner—and then they wanted to make sure my wife was making it all happen. Fuck that. I would sue them before that happened. You're not going to tell me when I fight and when I don't fight. Sure, the Astros didn't want to. I get it. On the field, they were all chirpy, but I would see them in street clothes, and they just put their heads down.

Major League Baseball sometimes doesn't get it. If people want to fight, they are going to fight. And if you put these two teams in the same hotel, after all that happened, we're probably going to fight. It's an emotion. It's part of the whole deal. It's a microcosm of how misguided MLB can be.

But when we're talking about the greater good, the most important piece of the pouting puzzle came in a very unexpected form. I should have known, but I didn't. Baseball should know, but it often doesn't. It turns out that when you're just being yourself, that's when you can have the most impact. That was certainly the case this time around.

First came the social media memes. Then people randomly started asking me to pout. Restaurants. Playgrounds. Drive-throughs. Airports. "Joe, do the pout!" It all caught me off guard. But I'll tell you what, my four-year-old son, Knox, sure liked it. At every turn—when I would make the excuse that I was saving the expression for a lucrative NFT and thereby couldn't possibly pose in such a manner (which was a nice way of simply not wanting to wear out what had been an authentic moment)—Knox would gladly jump in. He loved pouting. And he loved the fact that his dad had brought such an exercise into the mainstream. T-shirts were made. Videos surfaced. And, for maybe the first time, my son truly got ahold of the fun that can come as a result of baseball.

Here is the reality: As of 2021, only 7 percent of Major League Baseball's television viewership consisted of fans under eighteen. We need to get kids in the door. In my son's case, the simple image of a pout paved the path.

For others, including Jonas Never, it served as a reminder that baseball has a way of bringing us along in its own subtly whimsical way.

As a Southern California kid growing up a fan of the Dodgers and ultimately living the life I did—including as a relief pitcher for the University of California-Riverside—I knew Jonas *got* the game. He looked for those memorable moments within each of the nine innings. In this case, he found one of those slap-in-the-face, baseball-is-awesome instances while flipping through television channels in an Atlanta hotel room. The Dodgers were on, so he was watching.

What Jonas saw had an immediate impact.

This was a guy whose works included iconic portraits capturing LeBron James and the late Kobe Bryant and Anthony Bourdain. They were greats. I was a relief pitcher. But for Jonas, when something hits, it hits. What he saw on TV hit.

He immediately ran out into an Atlanta rainstorm, bought a canvas, and started to paint. That piece of art wasn't the pout, but just me yelling at Correa over my shoulder and the words "Nice Swing Bitch" in the background. That was posted on Instagram, where my teammate Justin Turner took notice. Next thing I knew, JT was showing me Jonas's next creation—the beginning of a mural on the side of Floyd's 99 Barbershop on the corner of Sunset and Parkman.

"Is that big?" I asked Turner when he showed me.

"Are you kidding me? It's on the side of a building," he said.

"This man definitely deserved a wall," Never wrote on Instagram.

I don't know about that, but I do know that fans deserve this sort of reminder.

When the mural was done, I went to celebrate its completion with Jonas, agreeing this one time to break out the pout for the photographer. It was the least I could do. To see the reaction not only of Knox, but the fans—many of whom were regulars at Dodger Stadium, which resided just a couple miles away—hit me. It still blows my mind.

I can be walking down the street with some of the most famous baseball players in the world, and fans will yell, "Hey, Joe . . ." and then throw the exaggerated frown my way, followed by a smile and high five. As a reminder, I'm an average-looking relief pitcher. But I am also someone who isn't afraid to be a human being while actually wearing a baseball uniform.

Having fun. Being yourself. They are novel concepts, and one our baseball-playing brethren have to start wrapping their arms around.

When the latest round of Major League Baseball labor strife was taking place prior to the 2022 season, there were plenty of predictions that this would be the final straw for sports fans when it came to giving baseball the benefit of the doubt. I never got that. It's why I felt compelled to make a very public plea during one of the lockout low points.

So, this—my mission statement—was published in the *Los Angeles Times* on March 3, 2022:

FIRST PERSON: JOE KELLY PLEADS WITH FANS TO "NOT FORGET ABOUT BASEBALL" AMID MLB LOCKOUT

A plea: Don't give up on baseball. It's too important.

I get it. You're knee-deep in the millionaires vs. billionaires conversation that has dominated this offseason, looking for the signs of baseball stirring to life—images of ballplayers in sunglasses tossing baseballs in the shadows of palm trees, talk of rookies who look promising or players who deserve second chances. But none of those trusty signs of spring are here because of Major League Baseball's lockout. I don't blame you. This lockout feels like the last straw and you're tempted to turn your back on the game. The usual criticisms of baseball have come bubbling to the surface. Baseball is slow, out of touch, selfish, steeped in traditions that no one even remembers anymore. Yes, I get it. The game has been trying to hold onto your loyalty for years now. This is it. Enough.

But it's time to take a breath and understand, deep down, that baseball is awesome, and the same critics who love to undermine America's pastime know this. They know baseball can inspire, delight and define three-quarters of a calendar year. They cherish the game, and that's why they take issue with the way things are being managed. Is it the money that is at stake here? No, it's the game itself that's at stake. And I—along with my friends from all corners of the sports and entertainment world—am on a mission to save it.

Baseball is boring, they say.

Of course they do. Ours has become the ultimate instant gratification society, and the idea of baseball, the thinking man's game, isn't exactly scratching where most sports fans are itching. I get it. I was the kid who didn't want to take time to read the book, instead simply dialing up the SparkNotes synopsis so I could move on. And that's exactly what is going on now.

For some, all the business and beauty of baseball needs to be summed up in sound bites, tweets, and Instagram stories. It's so much more, which is a lesson I have learned.

The life-changing, meme-able fights off and on the field. Releasing a tidal wave of emotions from the mound on the

World Series stage. "@#!&, yeah!" Defining lifelong relationships with late-October hugs on the Dodger Stadium field have meant everything. For me, that has all been because of baseball.

You might not think this is an emotional game. Too much standing around. Picking flowers in the outfield. Talk, talk, talk and wait, wait, wait. Then, boom! The heart rate goes up for a few seconds. Then the cycle starts all over again.

That's the knock. Okay. But let me tell you that baseball can elicit the kind of emotions life rarely presents. And just when you think you had figured out those feelings, along comes something you didn't expect.

I know. It has happened to me.

Baseball has allowed me plenty of wake-up calls. Maybe this is the time for one more for us all.

This should be the reminder that baseball is a book, not a sentence.

Baseball is different from any other sport, where often you can watch the last few minutes of a game and get the gist. The NBA? The NFL? The NHL? What you see is what you get. Nothing wrong with any of it. The fast pace, the tight focus on a moving object, the made-for-TV rhythms of the season—they're all tailor-made for today's fans. Baseball? It's a bit more complicated and that's okay. Baseball makes you think. It makes you talk. Questions are being asked and answered. Why is that player doing this or that? And when the answers do arrive, the world somehow always seems to be a little bit better of a place.

If you're patient enough, you can see that baseball is a combination of chess, ballet, a classroom, and cannon fire.

When you're watching bat flips, punchouts, home-run-robbing catches, and laser throws from the warning track, it's easy to remember all the feels. Bathing in news of collective bargaining agreements, not so much.

We can't let this conversation slip away; we have to be diligent here, work hard to open a path for more and more sports fans to understand the importance of what baseball represents. This isn't Amazon. I can't order up a dose of October postseason drama, drop it at your doorstep and simply quench your thirst for instant gratification. That's not how baseball works. And that's okay. It's better than okay.

So, why is this message important to me and my baseball-playing brethren? Because maybe this is a crossroads. The momentum of 2021 was great. Younger fans. More excitement. A genuine feeling that a new generation was starting to buy in. And now we're at a screeching halt, stuck with hype men for baseball in the form of labor-relation attorneys. Would I love to throw my mariachi jacket on [Commissioner] Rob Manfred and start turning those boardroom frowns upside down? Of course.

It's where we belong and for fans it's a place where we can forget about the job, the workplace, and the business end of life—and just be. Bring on the celebrations, colorful cleats and seven months of chaos. It's where players can be personalities, not just numbers. Let's not forget the pageantry of it all. We have to trust that when the game emerges once more it will be better than ever and that's because we'll appreciate it more. I sincerely believe that.

All I ask is that while we are waiting, don't forget why you care so much. Don't forget why you own that player's jersey.

Don't forget why you bring that baseball glove to the game. Don't forget why you felt compelled to ask those questions and get those answers. Don't forget why baseball is so awesome.

I haven't, and never will.

. . .

When writing this book, I found myself glancing back at those words and the period during which I wrote them. Sometimes we need reminders. Consider this one more.

The hope is that we can crack through the instant and the obvious and take the time to be seduced by baseball once again, or even for the first time if you were never sold on the game before.

My voice is just one of many, no more or less important than anybody else who has been touched by baseball, as evidenced by the words and stories relayed by others within these pages. But we all thought it was important to tackle the topic. Baseball is so important, in so many ways.

It's time to wake up. Baseball is waiting for you.

CHAPTER TWO

ON THE FIELD

Baseball is built on emotion. That's a fact.

The feeling of wanting to explode in just the right way at just the right time is what the whole experience is about. Swinging a bat. Throwing a ball. Bursting down a base path. Springing toward the perfect fielding position. The heart rate shoots up and the body follows in lockstep. And in between all those actions, there's the other side: controlling your emotions in order for your mind and body to ultimately take over.

The battle between nerves, muscle memory, memories, and excitement is an every-game, every-inning, every-batter, every-pitch thing. That is what this sport demands.

Tell me I'm wrong. Anybody who has ever played or even watched this game understands exactly what I'm talking about.

Unfortunately, these days we are so bogged down in the minutiae of finding the best data-driven, intricately designed, modern-day version of this mid-1800s creation that we forget where the game will always be rooted: between the white lines.

There needs to be pushback on some of the ways the game is played. No doubt. But before diving into all the issues and rule changes that have owned baseball conversations of late, it seems only right to remember that the ultimate driving force of the game—emotion—will never change.

In the words of renowned singer and songwriter—as well as Boston baseball-lover—Juliana Hatfield: "Baseball is more than a game. It's like life played out on a field." It's so true. And every once in a while, that reminder gets put on full display. Take April 11, 2018, for instance.

I have been in a lot of fights. I'm not proud of it. It's just the reality. It just happens. It happens in life. It happens on the baseball field. In life, in sports, in baseball, emotion boils to the surface. And often, that emotion has been simmering for years and years.

• • •

When I was eleven years old, my dad walked to the mound, waited until I came in from shortstop, and then pulled me off the field in front of all my friends.

There was the time I delivered a punch to Dad's chest that put him on his ass during a pickup basketball game with my brothers.

And that time I told my college coach I wasn't going to play as long as that drunk just beyond the fence kept heckling me. You guessed it. That drunk was my dad.

It wasn't like Dad didn't understand all the emotions that come with athletic achievement. He was, after all, on the last Vanderbilt football team to beat Alabama, catching two touchdown passes in that game at Tuscaloosa. But what we both came to understand was this: Chasing those feelings can be a fruitless exercise, particularly if any joy is replaced by anger along the way. For me, that was the uncomfortable reality. My father was an alcoholic who was pushing me to become something he wanted me to be. With every nudge, baseball became less important, as did my relationship with my father.

One of the staples of baseball is those father–son moments. I hope my story can offer a reminder that just because there might be a fairy-tale ending doesn't mean there aren't some really rough innings before that final out.

He embarrassed me too many times to count because of his addiction to alcohol. My outward answer was to push away from the game that was supposed to be bringing us together. Baseball was fun as a kid until it wasn't. Too much time. Too many practices. Too much travel. And too much Dad.

The low point? It was probably the day I punched him.

It really started during those college workouts, when he would show up drunk, putting on public display the image I had hoped wouldn't leave our house. A shell of his former self, having lost seventy pounds, victimized by the gallon of vodka he had introduced himself to first thing in the morning. There he was, standing by the fence and yelling until I couldn't take it anymore. I just walked off the field.

"I'm leaving," I told my coach, Doug Smith.

"Why?" he asked.

"My dad is here. He's an alcoholic and an embarrassment. I'm not pitching until he gets out of here."

Dad left. So, I came back and pitched.

You want to talk about embarrassment? Try pitching after something like that, knowing that his exit was just a Band-Aid on the problem. I truly believe those kinds of emotions have hardened me to the point of numbness for those trips to the biggest stage. Life on a postseason pitching mound was nothing compared to seeing my dad slumped over that fence.

Soon after that experience, my brothers and I decided to play some basketball with Dad. I thought he had sobered up. I was wrong. The combination of competition and anger was unfortunately going to take this to a place neither of us thought it would go.

"Fucking sober up!" I yelled while jostling with him on the court in the front yard of our house. Then I went in for a rebound. Dad, who was still stronger than the rest of us, decided he was going to take out some aggression of his own. We yelled. Back and forth.

"You can't handle it?" he said.

"You're a fucking drunk!" I responded. I was at my boiling point. I punched him.

It's funny, I don't remember much from those dark times with my dad, except for specific moments like the fight. Everything did become much clearer after. He truly began to sober up. He became a different person, the kind who meant everything to me at the top of the mountain.

. . .

Joe Torre—who was Major League Baseball's chief decision-maker when it came to determining who needed to pay what kind of price for baseball fights—had a great quote in *The Guardian*. When asked why there were so many melees in baseball compared to other sports, he responded: "In basketball, you're running all the time, in football, you're colliding at high speed, but baseball tightens the emotional screws without much chance to let off steam."

I get that.

You wait and wait and wait until sometimes you just don't feel like waiting anymore. That's how it works. And the other part of the equation is this: Hardly any baseball players have actually gotten hit in the face. I know. I asked.

I went around one spring training and quizzed my teammates: "Were you ever hit in the face?" Most guys said no, never. My next question: "Have you ever been in a fight?" and most say they haven't. That's mind-blowing to me. Shocking. I grew up different. I was an angry kid. Everyone else probably looks at me like I'm the odd one. The guy who has the stab wound. The guy who laid out his dad. But here's the thing about being in a fight that every one of those fisticuffs newbies needs to know: When you're in it, you're in it. You're fighting for a purpose and, if you aren't, then you don't stand a chance.

You've seen guys on a baseball field who want absolutely no part of a fight, even though it's going to define their lot in life on their team and maybe even the perception of their team as a whole.

For me, the emotion that comes with fighting is part of life. Why should it be any different because I'm in a baseball uniform? That's what we're talking about, isn't it? Being real as baseball players. Being human beings and not faceless, nameless guys existing under the cloud of unwritten rules.

I get it. Everybody is different.

I got into my first fight when I was eleven years old. It was nothing more than a case of being a wound-up kid who thought he had the only parents who were divorced. Back then it seemed like nobody split up. Now nobody gives a fuck. I was embarrassed and angry. And up until that moment, on a travel ball trip to Las Vegas, I really didn't know how angry.

It took a simple trigger, a bigger kid—a lot bigger than me—picking on a friend of mine, Billy. He was really tiny. We were all in the game room at the Sunset Station Casino, and this big kid kept picking on Billy and getting rough with him. Finally, the bully slid down this slide right after Billy and started picking him up, making my buddy fall to the ground.

I was like, "Get the fuck off of him!" I shoved him with my left hand and punched him right in his sternum area (because, once again, he was a giant). He started laughing, which pissed me off. So, in a matter of less than a second, I decked him. He walked out of there, eyes watering, bloody nose. He never told his parents, because he was embarrassed he got beat up by a kid my size.

That was it, my first fight. It wasn't anything more complicated than me thinking of another kid on my team.

That's how it worked as an eleven-year-old, and that's how it worked on the Fenway Park mound in Boston eighteen years later.

By the time the Yankees' Tyler Austin decided to run toward me on an April night in Boston, most people didn't know my story. They had no idea about my dad. They didn't realize there had been plenty of knock-down, drag-out brawls in my life. What they saw was a skinny relief pitcher who hardly looked the part of someone who fell into that minority of baseball players who had actually been hit in the face.

There was no history of me fighting on a baseball field. That changed in an instant in the middle of the Fenway Park diamond. A lot changed on that night. Actual emotions on the field will do that.

Before we get into what happened, let me just say this: You don't want to be too angry in a fight. I've come to learn that. You have to channel your anger so you can slow things down.

If I fight someone who is angrier than me, I know I'm going to win because I understand how to slow things down. I can react faster. I throw 100 miles per hour. I'm 180 pounds. You know my quick-twitch muscles are quicker than anyone I have ever fought so I'm going to get more punches in. I just feel like I have all the advantages.

That was certainly the case that night.

The situation was this: When I took the mound for the seventh inning of that game against the Yankees, I was probably the least popular player on the Red Sox. I had blown the very first game of the season—giving up four runs while getting just one out—and had pitched just three times since. Things were good for everybody else on the team. We had won nine straight after the Opening Day loss against the Rays, and we were rolling. But in the eyes of many, I was the guy who supplied the only black mark on an otherwise pristine start to the season. It's also why I was the guy to come in pitching when we were down by four runs to the Yankees.

That didn't matter to me. What mattered to me was the moment. It wasn't all that different from sticking up for Billy or my wife or anybody else in my family. This has always been one of the things I love about baseball, how it could mirror life and all the ups and downs that go with it. There is no other sport that does that like baseball. That's a fact.

Four innings before I came in, Austin—a guy whose six-foot-two, 220-pound frame offered the physical stature most athletes would sign up for in a heartbeat—slid into second base. The problem was that by the time he began his descent into the bag, the baserunner was plummeting toward the knees of our second baseman Brock Holt. That was a no-no. Austin also chose to lift his leg just enough to cleat Brock's leg. Another no-no. Some unwritten rules are dumb. But frowning upon this kind of slide is *not* one of them, and we knew it. Benches cleared. We ran in from the bullpen. People yapped a bit, and then everyone went their separate ways.

It just so happened that the left side of Austin's rib cage met my sixth pitch of the game about an hour later.

My life as a Red Sox player was about to change.

Austin pounded his bat on the ground after absorbing the 98 mph fastball, started walking toward me, and then . . .

Rule No. 1 for me is not to be embarrassed in front of a lot of people. He was not going to make me look like an idiot, especially after he'd just made this scene and started acting like a big baby. That triggered me. This guy wasn't going to have a choice: He was coming out to fight me. You're not going to do all of this without some consequences.

"Let's go!"

That's what I yelled at him as he approached, because that was what was going through my mind. I was going to make sure this happened. Go look at the video. Go look at my eyes. At that point, it wasn't about baseball, who was watching, who was screaming, or anything else. Sure, I might have had an ERA (earned run average) over seven when I threw that pitch, but in my mind, the Red Sox had found the right guy at the right time. That's why I smiled, just for a second. In my mind, I had been in this sort of situation a million times. I don't think the same could be said for Austin.

Then came the basics: Use my athleticism, don't let him wrap me up, and then let him carry himself into a position he didn't want to be in. I felt very comfortable.

I had no idea where Austin was raised. I didn't know his history. But I do know that most of these guys who aren't from

Latin American countries haven't had to fight as I had. Again, not a lot of these guys want to get punched in the face, and if you've never been punched in the face, you don't know how to react when you do get smacked. That's why baseball players tackle one another in these things. That's what Austin tried to do, which was absolutely not a surprise.

But for me, this was about more than just getting an attaboy for being a Red Sox player who punched a Yankee. This was that emotion I was talking about. For Austin and a bunch of the players on the field that night, it had built up in just a matter of hours. For me, it was a lifetime. Divorce. Alcoholism. All those previous scraps. I was prepared for this because of it all.

People think I'm crazy. I don't feel that way. I just do things others won't. I guess I'm wired differently. I think the same things other ballplayers do. I just might act on those thoughts a bit more. That sort of thing—embracing the chaos of a fight in front of forty thousand people—isn't for everyone, especially for baseball players who don't view it as part of the bargain. It is for me.

A few weeks after that night of on-the-field chaos, the feeling hadn't gone away. How did I know? Easy. While driving through Times Square with my agents, Sam and Seth Levinson, I spied Austin crossing the street.

"Let me out of the car!"

Something flipped in my mind, and we were right back on the Fenway Park field. I didn't care if it was in front of a bunch of tourists and a sea of police officers. I had unfinished business with Austin. Baseball and life were one and the same, with this bit of serendipity serving as the latest example. Sam and Seth didn't see it the same way.

"You're not going anywhere. Lock the door," they both yelled to the driver. While my mindset was singularly focused on finishing unfinished business, my agents were slapping me in the face with common sense. Slowly, I settled back into my seat and started coming to grips with the difference between the middle of a baseball diamond and the heart of one of the world's busiest intersections.

There was something else I became well aware of, thanks to those flying fists at Fenway: Fights are one thing, the fallout another.

. . .

When I stood up for Billy in Vegas, that meant a lot to both of us. When I punched my dad, the path toward actually healing was finally paved. And when the dust from the Austin thing had settled, everything started changing.

First off, there was the team.

We were good before that fight at Fenway, but there had been something missing. How do I know? It was verbalized by my teammates. It was clear some of the guys had absolutely no problem mixing it up. Mitch Moreland. Rafael Devers. We all came from different backgrounds, but we had all been there before in our own ways. For others, it had to serve as a wake-up call. Good intentions aren't always good enough.

"You guys are fucking pussies. You're going to let Joe be out there by himself!" That was the outcry of one teammate after the scrap with the Yankees. There were other words of similar ilk.

It was part of a team meeting making it perfectly clear that some guys were slow to the fight. The punches landed. The final score. They didn't matter nearly as much as the lessons that needed to be learned in that uncomfortable clubhouse get-together. By the time we left that room, it was understood. We won eight in a row after that. Not a coincidence.

We knew how good we were. There were just a few missing pieces to the puzzle that were going to make us great. Fortunately, all it took was a fight with the Yankees two weeks into the season to start making the team fit together.

It's weird because, for a sport that eats up about seven or eight months of every year and encompasses at least 162 games, singular emotional moments like this can mean so much toward the end result. That's another thing that can be awesome about baseball.

In the next month, I went from zero to hero. News flash: Red Sox fans like it when you wallop a Yankee.

"Joe Kelly Fight Club" T-shirts became the souvenir stores' best-selling item, and all of a sudden people didn't mind so much that I had ruined their Opening Day. By the time we went to New York about a month later, those shirts were everywhere, which was crazy. Sometimes it takes months and months and months for a team to find its identity. The "Fight Club" thing wasn't only about me. It was about us. I loved it.

You can go to any Red Sox game years later and find a T-shirt reminding us all of the moment. Since then I have been asked who, exactly, is in the Fight Club. Well, I have five former teammates I'm inducting:

MITCH MORELAND: He was the first one who came to my defense in the Austin fight, and I have seen him off the field having a good wrestling match with more than a few guys.

CHRIS SALE: When he says something, he means it. He isn't going to beat around the bush and say something he's not ready to back up.

YADIER MOLINA: Yadi has two older brothers, so he has had to get into some scrums, and he is one of the best catchers of all time, which instantly shows toughness.

AUSTIN BARNES: Simply put, he's from Riverside, and I know he has been in his fair share of scrums.

DAVID FREESE: He is one of the strongest guys I have seen in baseball and has definitely been around the scenes when it comes to Royal Rumbles (the official kickoff to the WWE's WrestleMania).

They are reminders that reliability in this world of baseball is a powerful thing and an undeniable necessity.

I guarantee teams were afraid to play us not only because we were good, but because they were thinking, *Shit, this guy might throw at us and we'll have to fight.* That's good leverage to have.

It was us against the world, and we were winning.

Later, 198 days to be exact, the power of performance appeared once again, helping define all that we knew the 2018 Red Sox could be. This time the thrill of baseball was pushed to the forefront by one player—Nathan Edward Eovaldi, "Nate."

The emotion that can be found on the baseball field can come in so many ways, with the Yankees fight offering one example, and seven months of winning supplying plenty of others. But it was six innings of pitching into the wee hours of the Los Angeles night that left a collection of baseball players in awe. Sometimes great athletic achievements can amaze and inspire. But I have never witnessed anything like what we saw Nate do during Game 3 of the World Series.

How impressive was it? We lost, and we literally didn't care.

It didn't hurt that, despite falling into a 2–2 series tie with the Dodgers that night, there were no worries on our side. We knew we were a better team, and we knew we would eventually win in the best-of-seven series. That might sound cocky, but it's the vibe we possessed.

What trumped the final score was how one player stood out from fifty-one others that night.

About five hours after I had pitched a scoreless sixth inning, Nate—a quiet Texan in his early thirties whose body screamed fitness—walked off the field having pitched six innings of relief. He threw ninety-seven pitches (in relief!), with the last pitch finally punctuating the affair with a Max Muncy home run in the eighteenth inning. (For those wondering, those eighteen innings took seven hours and twenty minutes, with the press box serving eight hundred Dodger Dogs to the assembled media.)

Eovaldi stood on that Dodger Stadium mound, retiring one Dodger batter after another for eighteen outs despite pitching in the previous two World Series games. But that was just one piece of the picture. As those pitches started piling up, we were pulling for Nate to simply stop. We could tell even our manager, Alex Cora, wanted to pull the plug. The reason? We felt this was a man putting his career in jeopardy. It was too much.

Nate, who was scheduled to become a free agent after the season's end, had already undergone two Tommy John surgeries (intended to stabilize the elbow) and was emptying the tank well beyond what anybody thought was possible. He didn't care.

Eovaldi wasn't talking to anybody, and he certainly wasn't coming out of the game.

This was baseball heroism under a World Series spotlight. The rest of us on the Red Sox roster had morphed from baseball players to baseball fans.

The standing ovation in the clubhouse for Eovaldi after the game was all we could give Nate. What he gave us was something we all could hang on to for the remainder of our days—a feeling that encapsulated all that is good in baseball and all you could ask for when seeking inspiration.

Now, if we can just make the world see how this sport made such feelings possible.

• • •

Emotion and inspiration: check and check. Another box in baseball's amazing column is foundational tenets of the game—which were really established in 1845 by a volunteer firefighter and bank clerk by the name of Alexander Joy Cartwright of the New York Knickerbocker Base Ball Club—and how they have held up. Sure, we've done away with throwing the baseball at baserunners to secure outs. But the diamond-shaped infield, three-out rule, and other concepts have stood the test of time.

The twelve-page "Laws of Base Ball" document drawn up in 1857 by a group of East Coast baseball clubs laid it all out: Nine-inning games. Ninety feet between the bases. Nine players on a side. Sound familiar?

And, I'm sure in their own way, that first wave of baseball players were drawn by the same thrills we have been seduced by. No doubt somebody in that 1871 Philadelphia Athletics club was inspired by the performance of Count Sensenderfer, and

I'm sure the "Ledell Titcomb Fight Club" was some sort of thing back in 1886.

But the urge to alter what has always been is getting stronger by the day. We players can hear that, and we can certainly feel it as well.

When the average demographic of your fan base keeps creeping toward sixty-year-olds, with the world's attention span narrowing by the day, it's not rocket science: We have to take a step back and rethink what kind of rules will perfectly complement and highlight baseball's emotional foundation.

I have my thoughts.

SHOULD PITCHERS HIT?

Heading into the 2022 season, Major League Baseball finally ripped off the Band-Aid and instituted designated hitters for every team in baseball. I get it. It's hard to suggest that fans are flocking to the ballpark to watch automatic outs.

In the twenty years leading up to the rule that took the bat out of National League pitchers' hands, they had a collective batting average of .135, striking out in 42 percent of their at-bats. Not good. So, for the good of the game, I'm not really against it.

I do, however, think it's important to give a pitcher's perspective on the DH dynamic.

They might stink at it, but I haven't met too many pitchers who didn't like hitting. Adam Wainwright? Man, did he love it. Others, too. For them it was a good distraction from their task at hand. I was no different. And I did okay. Before they changed the rules, I managed fifteen hits in ninety-two at-bats, four of them actually coming in the form of doubles. But . . .

Yes, all the strikeouts from pitchers are far from memorable. But how about when the ball does hit the pitcher's bat in just the right way. I came to know that feeling in 2013 when I ripped an opposite-field double off then-Cubs starter Jeff Samardzija. Ninety-eight mph up and away, followed by a mild version of a bat flip. He didn't like it. So, next time I got up, that 98 mph fastball was directed at me. And that's another beauty of pitchers hitting—retribution can be direct, thanks to the inability to avoid the batter's box. The next time Samardzija got up, he got 98 mph up and in. Finally, our managers told us to knock it off.

Now, all of it is a thing of the past.

Also gone is all the strategy that came with trying to figure out exactly how long a pitcher should remain in the lineup. Double-switches when pitchers exit? I have seen plenty of skippers who simply can't get their head around it. It actually took some strategy and thought, which now is off their plate. Those are the times when former manager Sparky Anderson's words, "A baseball manager is a necessary evil," ring truer than ever.

Now, we're left with one guy, the Angels' Shohei Ohtani. He is an aberration, the starting pitcher who serves as a DH on his off days and does both jobs better than almost anybody else. Yet those who say he is opening doors for the next wave of two-way players are misguided. Clubs won't allow it. They bend over backward for Shohei because his talent demands it. Teams are simply too insecure to let players focus on both instead of specializing in one, killing any idea that we're on the cusp of a wave of hitters who pitch and pitchers who hit. We will just have to revel in the memories of Babe Ruth and random relief-pitcher opposite-field doubles.

It was a nice run while it lasted.

BRING ON THE ROBOT UMPS

I have nothing against umpires. I'm like some pitchers who know every little thing about who is calling the balls and strikes. Their tendencies, personalities, and histories—and I don't even know their names. That doesn't make it right; it's just me.

I do, however, have a pretty good idea of how and why a home plate umpire makes his decisions when raising his right arm for a strike call and letting it dangle for a ball. They mean well, but it is all undeniably an imperfect process. So, when we're talking about putting our best foot forward, doesn't having the consistency that comes with technology fall under that umbrella?

Let's get the calls consistently right, and bringing on the robots will do that. With humans, even though the parameters are the same, each umpire is different. That's why when you go to a website that grades such performances, none of them are ever the same. They're all missing calls, but in different ways. I just want it to be the same every time. I think we all do.

Bring on the robots!

When I face six-foot-eight Aaron Judge, if I'm painting just below his letters, umpires are calling it a strike. That's a no-doubt-about-it ball if I pitch just below José Altuve's letters. The strike zones change with every body type. That isn't right.

I will say this: Sometimes human interaction makes life a bit more amusing. That part of the game—with players and managers and umpires going back and forth with anger and animosity—is slowly exiting the equation. First it was replay, which took away the knock-down, drag-out on-field arguments. They pop up every now and again, but not nearly as much as when the crowd would be woken up in the middle of a blow-out with a nose-to-nose, spit-flying disagreement. Now we will

37

be stripped of the last remaining room for interpretation—disputing balls and strikes.

I have never been one for yelling at the home plate umpire, voicing my displeasure with his decisions. Pitchers have to think long and hard before they go that route, considering the grudges that might be held. But sometimes it's hard to reel it in. What I default to aren't words, or even eye-daggers. My preference is to appear dumbfounded. Kind of like, "Huh?! You will have to excuse me, but I don't fully understand your ineptness." That might lead to the kind of embarrassment that makes them think twice about getting it wrong next time.

Unfortunately, last I checked, robots don't get embarrassed. So be it. We can live without a little less human emotion in order to actually get these calls right.

THE VOICES IN MY HEAD

Speaking of technology . . .

So, when I first heard about this PitchCom thing—the wireless speaker that relays the signs audibly through a touchpad wristband the catcher controls—I thought there was no way that was going to become part of my deal. While some guys were swearing by it, I kept coming back to one flaw—how was the catcher going to really emphasize the intention of whatever pitch he was calling?

For me, that was a big deal.

I came up with one of the best catchers ever to play baseball, Yadier Molina, guiding me through games not only with his signal-calling, but also with the kind of subtle body-language-driven explanation of each pitch that a young pitcher like me really needed. A fastball is a fastball, but a fastball called by Molina with a subtle pump of the catcher's mitt and sternness in putting down that one finger was everything. This contraption was going to take that away.

But, like a lot of pitchers I know, I started coming around on the idea of the button pushing. Where at first it seemed like something had to go wrong with the process, the more the 2022 season went by, the more it became just a matter-of-fact way of life.

Somebody on your staff voices each pitch and location, and then it's put in as a recording to be played when the corresponding button is pushed by the catcher. Tiny speakers are given to the pitcher and middle infielder and center fielder, who all use the information for positioning purposes. For Spanish-speaking guys, there is Spanish. For those from Japan, you have Japanese. And if a pitcher really wants, he can get additional customized messages along the lines of what I was initially yearning for. "Throw your best shit-kicking fastball right now!"

There are going to be bumps in the road, as was the case when Red Sox shortstop Xander Bogaerts switched speakers with his pitcher Hirokazu Sawamura and ended up having to learn the Japanese word for "splitter" on the fly. And there is always the concern that runners on second will be able to hear the speaker of a middle infielder if close enough.

But for the most part, baseball got this one right.

The device even led me to the innovative side of my personality, figuring out that I could fasten it to the inside top front portion of my hat—instead of the usual spot atop the ear—to give some surround-sound action to the whole equation.

What truly sealed the deal for me, however, was that it allowed for an unexpected benefit: I no longer needed to wear my glasses.

It might seem like a small thing, but getting rid of my specs was a big deal considering the challenge that bad lighting, humidity, or rain always presented. With PitchCom, I didn't need to see the catcher's signs, which was the only reason I wore goggles in the first place.

Lesson learned: Change can be good. Welcome to the baseball-balancing act.

LET'S SPEED THINGS UP

First off, let's get this out of the way: I hate being hot, and I despise sweating, so what I'm going to say is admittedly selfish: Baseball has to start picking up the pace a bit.

Some managers, coaches, and players will try to tell you they're so immersed in the game that they can't tell the difference between a three-hour and a four-hour game. I call bullshit. I know I can. Maybe it's because life in the bullpen can drag, being so isolated from the action and not really immersed in the decision-making cauldron. Still, I have to imagine everyone feels it when riding out the stops and starts of a baseball game for as many minutes as back-to-back, full-length movies.

Even on that drama-filled night when Eovaldi had all our mouths agape for six innings, doing so on the biggest stage a baseball season could offer, you could feel the length of the game. In some ways, it is an unavoidable reality for our game. In others, there are tweaks to be made.

Especially on those hot days in the bullpens and baseball fields with nary a bit of shade to be found, I'm all in when it comes to exploring some alterations.

The caveat here is that we can't get too consumed with the actual time allotted for each baseball game. One of the romantic parts of baseball is that it has no time limit. The game runs its course and doesn't rely on the tick-tock of a clock. Nobody is going to start printing up bumper stickers if fifteen minutes gets shaved off the average time of a game.

There is one word, however, that should resonate every time this topic comes up: *urgency*.

You have to make it feel like the windows between actual bits of activity are getting smaller. It might be a three-hour game, but for the majority of those 180 minutes, you should be reacting based on what has happened and strategizing for anything that lies ahead.

Let's start with the pitch clock.

I'll admit, it will be hard for me, but I will have to learn. I'm not fast when it comes to getting the ball and getting back in for another pitcher. I'm not alone. That's just the way we have been allowed to do it all these years. I've gotten slower as time has gone on because, to be perfectly honest with you, I like to enjoy my time out there. I'm only out there for one fucking inning. And, once again, I don't want to be sweating, because I *hate* sweating. Oh, well.

I think guys will be okay, but it's more on the hitters than the pitchers. When they were doing this pitch clock in the minor leagues in 2022, the clock was fourteen seconds and hitters were told they had to be in the box with nine seconds to go. Good luck telling major leaguers that, and good luck enforcing it when they push back.

The problem is that MLB has already tried to implement rules to speed things up. They do it for a while, it's fine a few people, and then it goes away. Case in point—in 2016, there was a big to-do about telling hitters to keep one foot in the batter's box in between pitches. That's still a rule, but watch any game and tell me how many times hitters venture outside the box without any repercussions. A ton. They don't enforce it at all. We have to remember this sort of thing any time these changes are implemented.

Still, we have to try something and can't be stubborn about not trying things. We can't be hypocrites. Put the whole adding-a-runner-on-second-in-extra-innings under that tent, as well. It's a different kind of baseball—a better kind of baseball.

I would also go so far as changing all games to seven innings. This comes back to the urgency conversation. Those seven-inning doubleheaders were awesome. I remember hating going to play Division 1 baseball because it went from seven innings at the high-school level to nine innings. Those two extra innings were tough to take. It felt so fucking long.

It can be brutal going from those seven-inning doubleheaders to the regular nine the next day. Those two extra innings can be a big deal. You're already burned out from playing two games in one day, and then you get the next one and you immediately think, *Damn, we have two more innings to cover?* It's like a tease. Seven innings all the time would be ideal.

Looking back, it's amazing how arbitrary it was that nine innings became the law of baseball, considering it simply lined up with the nine players the 1856 New York Knickerbockers decided to play with. It stuck, and don't think for a second—despite my disapproval—it's going to go anywhere.

Baseball is built on records and history. Play two fewer innings, many of those markers have to start from scratch. That is never going to happen. It's also a sport constructed on money. Playing a game that includes two fewer innings means you need fewer players, and starting pitchers will become almost obsolete. Every game will be a flood of relievers, matching up three hitters at a time.

Dare to dream.

THE SHIFT? GOOD RIDDANCE

Shifting fielders? See ya!

I have kept track of it on my phone, the times the shift has helped me and the times it has hurt me, and it's only confirming my hunches. I will be better off without it. I understand why teams value it, with models constantly pointing at hits that were taken away. The art of hitting the ball up the middle has gone out the window. But I can't help how I feel. Thankfully, baseball's decided to insist on semi-traditional positioning and see where we land.

As pitchers, these shifts have always been tough to get our heads around, especially when watching what would be a routine ground ball to shortstop head into left field for a hit. And there are also those instances where a hitter steps to the plate, we shift everyone around, and I just know the guy is going to hit it where we aren't. A lot of times, if I'm aware of it, I will turn around and move guys back on my own, but then it becomes somewhat of a pissing contest.

The big question is why more hitters haven't taken advantage of the gifts we were giving them.

All it would have taken all these years is the ability to put down a bunt. A simple bunt.

It seems ironic now, looking back at a passage in the *Brooklyn Eagle* newspaper from 1873 when the bunt was invented, explaining that "The object of the batsman is to reach first base, and if by any style of hitting he can send the ball fairly on the field . . . he earns his base by skillful scientific hitting."

And that same year, the *New York Clipper* newspaper wrote that this innovation required "the most skillful handling of the bat, and a quick eye and a steady nerve, besides."

It sure seems if this day and age of baseball analysts got ahold of something with that sort of description, they might prioritize it. Nope. Just keep trying to hit those home runs. So, why haven't they tried to reintroduce the art of bunting when these shift-induced gifts are given to them? Maybe hitters have fallen into the same trap that society has led us to, obsessed with instant gratification and simply believing bunting is flat-out boring. Or maybe they just can't do it.

Obsessing over launch-angle analytics isn't conducive to bunting. And then there is the biggest reason for the unwillingness to simply push a ball ten feet the right way: embarrassment. If a guy tries to execute the simple act and fails, it's embarrassing, and as we know, that is baseball's most painful emotion.

We gave the shifts a whirl, now thanks to the new rules from MLB's Joint Competition Committee, it's time to move on.

UNWRITTEN RULES CAN BE DUMB, UNTIL THEY'RE NOT

I guess other sports have rules that aren't documented by their leagues but are understood from player to player. But it sure seems like baseball's list is a whole lot longer than any other of its ball-playing brethren . . . by a long shot.

Maybe it's because there are far more ins and outs when it comes to getting to the finish line of a baseball game than in other sports. Every single mandate can't possibly be documented. And perhaps the sport is already so busy fending off critics when it comes to the written rules that these fringe regulations—otherwise known as the unwritten rules—continue in ambiguity.

This I understand: You better know these invisible regulations, and you also better be able to back up your actions when either following along or turning your back on them.

A good chunk of the list involves how to act when one team has a big lead. We're talking about seven or eight runs maybe from the seventh inning and on. For instance, the idea of the team holding the advantage attempting to steal bases is no good. There's no need and it's just selfish. But another one that some might bristle at—swinging at a 3–0 pitch with such a lead—I have no problem with at all, because you actually have the chance to get someone out on 3–0. Thank you. I have never been mad at someone swinging at 3–0. It has never bothered me. Stealing with a giant lead? Yes. But 3–0 swings with a giant lead? Nope. Nobody should ever be mad at that.

Back in 2021, when the White Sox's Yermín Mercedes took the Twins' Williams Astudillo (a position player who was pitching) deep on a 3–0, 47 mph fastball while Chicago was up eleven runs, everyone got upset. Welcome to baseball. You have to have a pitcher and you have to have a hitter. And, no matter what the score, they both have a job to do.

Anyway, 3–0 counts can be tricky. If there is nobody on base, sure, I'm going to throw a fastball right down the middle. But if it's Fernando Tatis, I'm throwing a curveball. I would rather walk him every time. For hitters, the 3–0 count is a gift, as the collective .379 batting average and 1.739 OPS (on-base plus slugging) in Major League Baseball over the last ten years would suggest. It's the hole we dug as pitchers, and no matter what the score, it's the hole we have to dig ourselves out from.

And when batters do hit those home runs, I have absolutely no problem with them pausing, bat flipping, and enjoying. For years, the invisible book of unwritten rules suggested batters pimping homers should be frowned on. Respect the pitcher. Respect the game.

News flash: If you really want to respect baseball, understand that we need more of that personality. Pimp away. Take a minute rounding the bases. Pitchers, throw your hats up in the air. Pump your fists. Whatever you want. If somebody hits a home run off me, I'm already fucking pissed. The hitter doing whatever he's going to do won't make me any angrier.

The great thing is that I feel I'm finally not alone in accepting that bat flips aren't necessarily a bad thing. In the last few years, players have started coming to grips with the act as a chance to prop up the game's personalities. When I was a rookie, nobody bat flipped. I had never seen a bat flip, ever. High school. College. Pros. Ever.

I love Max Muncy's bat flip, because he looks so disgusted when he does it, like he's saying, "Finally!" He barely does anything with the bat, but he propels it straight down, as if to say, "Get this out of my fucking hands! Finally!"

In fairness, I can't remember a lot of hitters slowing down or even bat flipping after hitting a home run against me. I'm guessing that's because they think I'm going to nail them if they do. Which brings us to one of the meat-and-potatoes chapters of the unwritten rule book—the art of retaliation.

You hit our guy. We hit your guy. That's fair. You slide late into one of our infielders, potentially ruining his career. A retaliatory pitch is also fair. At least aiming for ribs or below. But if it's for something crazy—like making someone bloody or some off-the-field shit—it's wherever you get him.

When Tyler Austin slid into Brock, I aimed for his ribs. I was just protecting my teammate. In cases like that, if you have good leaders on a team, they will quickly say something like, "Let's get 'im!" It's not usual that a manager walks down and issues the directive. Players know, or at least they should.

When Manny Machado slid into Dustin Pedroia in 2017, we all understood. The first pitcher to see him the next day should hit him. But we kept missing our chances, whether it was guys not willing to do it or guys not being able to execute the task at hand. We had to wait until we got home when Chris Sale basically said (without actually saying it): "You guys suck. I'll show you how to do it." We were all pissed we couldn't take care of it when we should have taken care of it, but we also knew if there was one guy who understood what was what, it was Sale. We weren't wrong.

Machado at the plate. Chris on the mound. First pitch. Right at Manny's knee, just missing behind. Message sent. That's how it works. Did I mention that Pedroia's career basically ended on Machado's late slide?

It was all a reminder that these sorts of progressions aren't just for shits and giggles. There has to be some semblance of accountability, and baseball affords us the opportunity to remind us all of such things.

For me a smaller example is a guy calling time-out really late, just as I'm about to deliver the ball. That pisses me off. When that happens and I have to follow through with the pitch, I'm nailing him. Free pitch. Hopefully they will learn their lesson. Again, it's about accountability.

I will say that this long list of unwritten rules can get a bit silly. Not talking to a starting pitcher while he's throwing a no-hitter? What if he is a talkative guy and enjoys the conversation? Want to bunt during a no-hitter, just use common sense. Would you be bunting earlier in the game? No. So, don't bunt for the sole reason of not embarrassing your team.

The dos and don'ts never seem to end, with the old guard sometimes getting so riled up and some of the newbies not fully understanding why such traditions are in place.

Baseball better start building some generational bridges.

. . .

I get a kick out of these fans who have been watching the game for forty years screaming and yelling at their televisions. "Just let them play! Stop with all the substitutions and smarty-pants moves!"

If they only knew. You know what? We should let them know.

The world of baseball technology is changing the game and not enough fans have a clue what the hell is going on. We have to change that. Open the curtain for even the most casual of fans. Let's give them all the information that even some major league teams are still trying to get their heads around.

Simply put, there is a reason the same teams make the playoffs and win so many games, and it isn't about payrolls or superstars. It's about being smart. It's why people are screaming at the Rays for having a roster full of low-paid, shitty players, yet the Rays go out and win a hundred games. We have to start doing a better job integrating some education within the entertainment for those consuming this game.

Why is Joe Kelly coming on to face the meat of the batting order instead of the closer? Well, his curveball grades out at a spin rate of 3,400 when the other guy clocks in at just 2,400. The teams know this. It's why the Dodgers signed me and then used me in those big spots. The old man yelling to the baseball gods was probably screaming for our closer, Kenley Jansen. Well, he got a one-year contract, and I signed for two years with rejuvenating biceps. The teams knew what was what. Now it's time to let the fans in.

Have someone in each and every broadcast telling the fans the story behind the story as the game unfolds. This shouldn't be secretive. It should be part of our solution.

Believe me, I know how eye-opening it can be. When I went to the Dodgers, I was blown away by how much technology they were rolling out. They know how you tip pitches. They know how your ball spins. If you play at Dodger Stadium, they know everything about you. And I have come to discover they are far from being alone in the quest for next-level angles and execution.

From what I understand, the Giants actually have facial recognition software at their ballpark. Facial recognition software! And why not? It's legal and downright genius. One more team that gets it. When they are winning all those games and everyone sits somewhat befuddled after digesting their roster, we know what's going on. They are investing in technology, sifting through the data, and then putting their players in perfect positions to succeed.

Why can't we help explain to the fans why this is happening instead of simply thinking it's a product of good fortune?

Will the teams be paranoid to share such information? Maybe a little bit. But the reality is that everyone can access it with a little effort and monetary investment. And if this does become part of the baseball-watching experience, so much can change.

"What the fuck is the manager doing?" can quickly transform into, "Oh my God, now it makes so much sense!" That's what they will be saying. Doesn't that sound like something baseball might want to hear?

Let's give all baseball fans what they want, even if they don't realize quite yet that they want it.

There is some fixing to do, so let's get to it.

CHAPTER THREE

THE CLUBHOUSE: INSIDE OUR WEIRD WORLD

I wanted a neck tattoo. I wanted to shave my head. I wanted to put people in jail. My dream, going back as far as I can remember, was to be . . . an undercover narcotics agent.

Baseball player? No thanks.

Almost every kid I played with dreamed of wearing a baseball uniform well into adulthood. Not me. I was fascinated by living that bust-the-bad-guys life, the one thick with the kind of adrenaline I imagined those dudes had. Maybe it was because of my own family's history with addiction and all the trouble that came with it, or perhaps it was simply figuring out how the mind works on both sides of the law.

I still want to be that guy. My wife tells me it's no longer an option, considering everyone in California will know who I am.

I told her it's nothing a shaved head won't take care of. Her next response is a bit more definitive: "Sorry. You have kids."

I can't help who I am, how I think, or what has driven me to this point. I always said that if someone was hurting my family and I had to kill that guy, I wouldn't blink an eye. I would sleep as soundly as if I just played a baseball game, as if I just pitched a shutout. Some people are built that way, and others wouldn't hurt a fly. I'm a hybrid. I have met people crazier than me, sure. Guys who make you think, *Damn, that's nuts!* I'm somewhere in between that and the majority of guys wearing a big-league baseball uniform.

Why am I even mentioning this? Because when you walk into a major league clubhouse, it can be the most eclectic, bizarre, and unique work environment known to humankind. There is simply nothing like it. So many different personalities coming from so many different corners of the globe. And, to top it off, you're around these people twice as much as you're around your own family.

The aspiring narco agent from Corona, California, is just one of many. That's what makes this baseball-playing world we live in so spectacularly special.

The rooms—or clubhouses—we inhabit aren't usually all that different or interesting. The home teams have next-level luxury, complete with captain's chairs, safes, and snacks galore to go along with lockers that are oftentimes double the size of those residing in the visitors' clubhouse. A lot of times veterans can pick which teammates they want on either side of them, with the real superstars oftentimes being afforded multiple lockers to spread out their possessions and perfumes.

But when you talk about the dynamic that comes with baseball clubhouses, you aren't talking about the furniture. You're beginning and ending with the personalities. Consider this: Of the 975 players on Opening Day rosters for the 2022 season, 28.2 percent hailed from outside the United States, representing twenty-one different countries or territories.

That's a lot of languages, a lot of paths, and a lot of personalities.

When I walked into my first clubhouse as a major leaguer—exactly two years and one day after I left my life as a college baseball player in the rearview mirror, thanks to being taken as the ninety-eighth overall player by the Cardinals in the 2009 MLB Draft on my twenty-first birthday—I didn't grasp this world I was entering.

That day in St. Louis is just a blur. I was in awe and completely clueless. All I knew was that guys like Yadier Molina, Lance Berkman, and Adam Wainwright were suddenly in the same room I was, and I guessed getting ready for the same game I was preparing to play in. Rules. Regulations. Rituals. None of it had really hit home. I look back now and am amazed how simplistic I had made such an ultimately complicated place.

Then, as time went by, I started talking to people and learned there was more to this room. There was more to baseball. This was our damn near perfect game, and day in, day out, I was soaking in all the reasons why.

What I found was that the vast majority of major league players had lived through some sort of struggle on their way to this point. And we're not talking about swinging and missing or giving up home runs. It was more along lines of shit that I had to navigate.

For me, I wanted to play baseball to escape the reality at home. I looked forward to the tournaments and the grind down on the diamonds. I didn't want to go home. My parents were divorced. My dad was an alcoholic. My brother was a heroin addict who just got out of prison. I didn't want to see all that. I was able to get out of the house, go down to the field, and focus on myself, taking all that anger out through the game of baseball. Striking guys out. Competing. It all felt good. And it ultimately led me to the majors.

The more guys I talked to, the more I heard stories with at least a hint of struggle to them. Theirs might not be identical to my deal, but there were similarities. This shit was hard, and I'm not talking about the sore muscles or the wind sprints. This is about the real struggles, the ones that made them men, no matter where they were from.

I think back to how naïve I was. I probably wasn't alone.

My idea of life in the major league inner sanctum was one built on an immediate impression. Just a bunch of guys playing the great game of baseball making a shit-ton of money. Maybe my myopic view of this world was born from having a very short runway to life as a professional baseball player, thinking up until my twentieth year on this planet that my calling was to sell drugs and potentially shoot people—all for the sake of law enforcement, of course.

I expected I would go to college, get my degree in psychology, maybe make some money playing pro baseball for a while before ultimately landing in the world of bulletproof vests. Deciphering the dynamic of a baseball clubhouse really wasn't on my radar.

I learned that until we're hit with the realities that come with pro ball, baseball can be pretty generic, at least on the surface. I might have had one or two kids on my college team who spoke Spanish, but that was it. It was the same in all the other teams we played. The focus is so much on just trying to get noticed. Sure, there are classes and, yes, some of your teammates come from different parts of the country. But, for the most part, college baseball was just an extended version of AAU. I certainly wasn't walking into our University of California, Riverside, locker room worried about how each corner of the room was going to get along. My thing was trying to navigate how to pitch, which I hadn't done since I was twelve years old. And once I realized that was going to work—winning the conference's Freshman Pitcher of the Year—then I just wanted to do whatever I could to get my life-changing chunk of money.

In hindsight, it's amazing how trying to become a baseball player can bring out the selfishness in someone.

Ultimately, that's another lesson this game should douse us with. This preeminent, statistically driven venture is actually the most dependent on human interaction and selflessness. Remember: February. March. April. May. June. July. August. September. And, it is hoped, October. That is nearly three-quarters of a calendar year during which a Major League Baseball player sees his coaches and teammates far more than his family. In other words, you better prioritize getting along with those guys.

I'm not going to lie. I was no different than a lot of these aspiring ballplayers. This was about my own deal. Take Draft Night, for instance.

June 9, 2009. It was not only the day I was planning on becoming a first-round draft pick—setting me up for life when it came to the checkbook—it was also my twenty-first birthday. In hindsight, that was an unfortunate combination.

The plan was for me to invite all my friends and family to Oggi's, a restaurant near where the Angels play, to celebrate my twenty-first year on this planet, along with my new life as a first-round Draft pick. Well, half of that equation worked out.

By the time the Draft was kicking off, my birthday party was already in full swing. Shots. Beers. You name it. The only thing that was missing was my name being called by a team. First round? Nothing. Supplemental round? Nothing. That's when the embarrassment—and the alcohol—started kicking in.

By the time the second round got underway, my selfishness—and my twenty-first birthday—had kicked in. That's when I got a call. It was from the Angels, the team just a few miles from my house. They wanted to know how much of a signing bonus I would need to sign considering I still had the option of going back to school. Millions and millions, I told them. It might have well have been *billions*. Whatever. I was blowing off a chance to play down the road because my loyalties had turned away from baseball and toward my party. Deep down, I had let selfishness get the better of me. Baseball isn't built on instant gratification. I should have known.

Eighteen picks after the Angels turned their backs on me and took pitcher Patrick Corbin, the Cardinals called. By then I was in full "fuck it" mode. I was already over the idea of using this night as my introduction to professional baseball, playing it all off like I was too cool for such concerns. I was being a dick. So, when the Cardinals scout called to say they were taking me, I was like, "Whatever!" I was going back to school, and I was going to become that no-doubt-about-it, first-round pick, immediately calling my college coach to tell him as much. For two weeks, I ruined that scout's life. He had told his bosses I would be an easy sign if picked at No. 98 and now I was threatening to waste a very valuable pick for St. Louis.

In the end, I signed for $340,000, about $110,000 less than what Corbin agreed to with the Angels. Blame it on the Jägermeister. Blame it on one of the first times baseball taught me the pitfalls of living that life with the always-dangerous, impatient, me-first mentality. That will never work in this game. I had a hundred grand less in my bank account, and a flurry of pissed-off family, friends, and baseball executives at the ready that night to help highlight the lesson.

Yes, I got my money and my opportunity. Nobody said that baseball doesn't have its shock-to-the-system snapshots. That's, in part, the promised payoff for all the waiting. But, as I noted before, this also isn't Amazon. You can't just order up immediate gratification and expect it to be delivered to your doorstep, dressed up in the kind of immaculate packaging that flushes away any unwanted anxiety.

Baseball makes you work for it, in so many ways. And that's why the payoff is so spectacular.

. . .

When you walk into that clubhouse, you better bring an open heart, open eyes, open ears, and open mind. Selfishness and rest-lessness don't work in this game. That hit me the moment I chose to take a hard look at my night at Oggi's, and then really rang true when my professional baseball journey kicked off a few weeks later in some place called Batavia, New York.

Back then, there was a serious lack of understanding when it came to what goes into making a Major League Baseball player. I, for one, was probably like most who envisioned the progres-sion going from getting a big check and living the good life while learning your craft a bit better in the minor leagues, and then—boom—you're a big leaguers. Nobody told me there were months of peanut butter and jelly sandwiches, crappy fields, and awful van rides.

I got to Batavia and quickly realized there were going to be a few more nightmares before my fairy-tale dream was going to come true.

Batavia was a nice enough town of about fifteen thousand folks, probably not all that different from other minor-league stops. It was notable enough to be referenced in both the 2001 movie *Summer Catch* and a season 8 episode of *The Simpsons*, with the Single-A team there carrying the catchy nickname of Muckdogs, a reference to the Genesee County mucklands.

But that didn't mean it didn't catch me—and plenty of my fellow professional, baseball-playing newbies—by surprise.

Playing next to the Genesee County Jail. A baseball field that wasn't even as well maintained as the majority of my Southern California haunts. Maybe sixty fans a game. It was all a kick in the face, and the only players who appeared to initially embrace the scene came from impoverished countries. I, however, was coming from the Big West Conference and Division 1 baseball.

Baseball is all about adjustments, maybe more than any other sport. This was my first big wake-up call when it came to understanding that.

Every minor leaguer has to face this warped world. For me it was making $680 every two weeks until I got to the big leagues. The fortunate thing is that, usually, you aren't living in high-rent cities or towns, but still there were times I was living with four to six teammates, some of us sleeping on couches. We almost always would rely on the food at the ballpark because eating out simply wasn't an option.

Here's the weird thing: I never really thought about it as it was unfolding unless somebody brought it up. I'm sure it is a shock for 80 percent of the guys who are thrust into the minor league world because they have an image of making money in professional baseball. But, for me, I always viewed it as a test, something that would make me stronger as a player.

The minor league experience in baseball is a microcosm of how the sport is juxtaposed against the likes of basketball and/or football. You're a good college player in those sports, and you're living the life right away. It is instant gratification. The fans know who you are, and so do your accountants. Very little waiting, and certainly no PB and J sandwiches. And when it comes to learning the importance of being a good teammate and a solid professional without the thumb of college coaches pressing down on you, other sports aren't anything like baseball.

I ultimately became grateful to baseball for making me wait.

There is no warning that kicking off a career will suck in so many ways for what feels like an eternity. I'm here to say, however, that the hardships and surprises were the foundation of my life as a professional. I suspect I'm not alone.

When you start to understand what this existence is all about, that's when the agony becomes enjoyment. Nobody is paying attention to how late you stay up. Your inevitable failures aren't put on display before forty thousand fans every night. And the joy of understanding that the world is a big place—filled with personalities, really good baseball players, and potential lifelong friends—is refreshed with each trip to the ballpark.

The minors is where I was indoctrinated into pitching like a pro. But it was also in that unfamiliar world that I learned to listen. For those wondering about the big, wonderful place that is a major league clubhouse, that is one of the most important skills to develop.

What any professional baseball player should learn once he starts living the life is something so simple, yet not nearly appreciated enough: Everybody has problems. Many times they are the kinds of problems that paychecks or fame can't resolve.

In many cases, the best medicine is simply baseball.

For instance, one of the most misguided questions a player can be asked is after a family tragedy when someone brings up the merit of actually showing up to the ballpark. That is a complete misunderstanding of how most of us are wired. This is the place where we know normalcy. We have worked our whole life to play in these games and live this existence. Take that piece of the puzzle away, and it can derail your mindset, adding to the depression that is already built in from whatever situation might have happened. Without the opportunity to stay in the safe haven that is a baseball clubhouse or field, you are tempting fate, perhaps leading someone down a darker road.

Playing the game of baseball is our drug. It's our dopamine. It's what makes us the happiest. Why don't people get this? We need baseball. As sappy as it might sound, it is our cure to what often ails us. It's the game. It's the teammates. It's the whole deal.

I'm not going to say I understood the power of the clubhouse community when I first came up to the big leagues. When I first walked into a dressing room as a major leaguer—coming on my twenty-fourth birthday exactly three years following that Draft-day wake-up call at Oggi's—I was in complete awe. There was no soaking it in.

When my Triple-A manager Ron "Pop" Warner called the day before to let me know I was getting the call, I put the phone down and thought: *What did he just say? What just happened? I think he said I am going to pitch in the big leagues, but I'm not really sure.* A day later, I arrived in St. Louis, but the cloud of disbelief still hadn't lifted.

There was Lance Berkman. There was Yadier Molina. There was Adam Wainwright. I was going to be playing baseball with them and for them. I don't know how others feel in such a situation, but for me that was surreal. All of it was a blur, which, looking back, kind of sucks. Now, I make it a point during these sort of soak-it-in instances to look at faces, whether wearing the uniforms or in the crowd. The passing of time has allowed me to pay attention to the little things, which I have learned can go a long way when living the life in a big-league clubhouse.

When a young guy has a rough day on the field, I make sure to play *Fortnite* or some other online video game with him to help take his mind off the problem. We talk about everything but the baseball-induced pain, dive into a whole separate round of competition, and, I hope, it allows for the anxiety to be put in the rearview mirror for at least a little while. It might not be a cure-all, but I can tell you it helps. That's the kind of thing I learned over time that can make a big difference.

I can tell you, when I first came up, that sort of thing simply wasn't an option for me. Guy has a bad outing? See you. Go figure it out on your own. Ten years ago, nobody was jumping in to play video games with the rookies. They had to earn the right to be acknowledged in the same light as players who had lived the life for a while.

Sit at your locker. Be quiet. Try going into the lunchroom and ask what is going on today . . . "Shut the fuck up!"

I never understood that.

As time went by, and I watched and listened, the old-school way of doing things seemed more archaic with each passing season. It has changed, no doubt. For the most part, rookies are viewed in the appropriate light—as a teammate who is going to help the team. It doesn't seem all that complicated, does it? So, why was it like that in the first place for all those years?

It's hardly the first time tradition and common sense butted heads in the world of baseball. But, for me, finding the correct approach when it comes to season-long human interaction should be a priority. That fascination I had trying to figure out the minds of those guys on the other side of the law and why they did what they did hadn't left just because I was playing baseball. The differences in brain construction and why they led people down such sometimes painful paths pushed me to understand those differences better.

One of the great developments in the game is the recognition by teams that—throughout this seven-month slog—there need to be actual coaches and experts with the players whose job it is to deal with the brain. There is also a far greater acceptance from the participants to use such people for talking through the emotional bear traps that exist. For a lot of these guys, this is a new phenomenon.

When I got to baseball, the wheels were already turning when it came to psychology.

There is so much to pick through regarding the mental intricacies of a clubhouse. But my fascination with human behavior centered around something that had smacked me in the face too many times—drug use.

I was fascinated not only by what led people to that world, but how it might be cut off at the pass. Why couldn't there be a way—a test—we give people early in life that could catch the propensity for addiction? Written test. Imaging. Anything. Maybe there is low dopamine, or somebody has next to no serotonin.

When kids start navigating their way through school, the adults in charge can usually tell if something is awry, but that simply leads to special classes or slightly alternative treatment. They know something is wrong, but rarely do they know why. I know. I lived it, just like so many others. Addiction, there's a lot of it in my family, and it has led to confrontations, heartache, and jail time.

I want answers. Much like watching the rookie wallow in his own misery, it doesn't seem to make any sense to watch the train wrecks unfold and not at least think about solutions.

And while we wait for more and better answers when it comes to figuring out how to cut off the downward spirals before they gain momentum, there has been a shift. Compared to when I first came up, the presence and use of drugs and alcohol simply isn't the same. Why? There are a couple of reasons.

First, players understand that the best-conditioned bodies are the ones that will make the most money and have an actual chance at winning. And the more success that comes with staying hangover-free, the more the mentality is passed along. That hasn't always been the case, but it sure is now. I guarantee the teams that are winning are the ones who are the most in tune with their physical state. In other words, they aren't getting regularly fucked up the night before.

Secondly, there's more to having a healthy lifestyle in a country that, for many ballplayers, is a foreign one. I have to give baseball credit for its clubhouse work in this regard, getting out ahead of a lot of stuff that had previously spiraled. For instance, when I experienced extended spring training with the White Sox in 2022—with a group made up mostly of teenagers from outside the United States—the team loaded them up on a bus and took them to Walmart to learn how to shop for the right kitchen staples. And when they got them back in their living quarters, the players were taught how to actually cook stuff that might keep them healthy. This simply wasn't in the equation a few years back.

Health has become so much better from the get-go in this game. I doubt anybody was making protein shakes for Mickey Mantle. And, most likely, nobody was giving Mickey shit for hitting it hard every night, either. Sure, he could handle it, but could the rookie two lockers down, who was looking up to him, follow in those footsteps? And part of that dynamic remains an issue.

Guys still are hesitant to tell their teammates to reel it in. That has to change.

There is, however, something that has been able to hold players accountable in recent years. Ironically, it is also one of the game's nuisances. That would be social media.

From where I'm sitting, there were way more drugs and alcohol before access to social media became a thing. Twice as much. Nowadays if you're doing those sorts of things, you have to be sneaky about it, with Twitter, Instagram, and Snapchat accounts at the ready, eager to document any little action or reaction. Before, you had to send it to TMZ. These days, each phone represents its own network news.

This is a very real thing, and one that is top of mind for anybody trying to build a career or (gasp) brand.

So, you might ask: Who is monitoring all of this? The mind-set. The preparation. The camaraderie.

You're talking about keeping it all glued together for all of spring training, 162 games, and then, hopefully, at least a few weeks into October. The manager and the coaches? They might lay the foundation, but when it comes to the actual execution of striking the all-important correct tone, that has to come from those playing the game.

In this respect, baseball is once again a unique experience.

Captains don't usually reside on baseball rosters. Sure, there are a smattering of players who have worn the familiar "C" in the same manner that hockey and basketball players are known for. But that has come and gone and for good reason. It's really hard to define just one guy in a world that is born from diversity, both in terms of geographic origins and professional responsibilities. How is a starting pitcher going to tell a middle-of-the-order slugger what's what? The ebbs and flows of a reliever's days don't exactly line up with that of the utility infielder. And then there are the language barriers, some of which can be bridged by bilingual teammates who might keep to themselves in most every other situation.

That doesn't mean there aren't leaders. Glue guys. You absolutely have to have them. And they don't need a "C" attached to their uniform to understand that.

When I was with the Red Sox, it wasn't as if David Ortiz had a stool ready for the middle-of-the-clubhouse, rah-rah speech. And when he was taking phone calls in between at-bats or easing his way down the first base line on random ground balls, nobody was screaming at youngsters to follow Papi's lead. But he was David Motherfucking Ortiz, and all the important stuff was filtered through him. That was always understood.

Wainwright. Dustin Pedroia. Justin Turner. It was accepted by everyone in our clubhouses that they, like Ortiz, understood the important stuff. And for a baseball team, finding those sorts of players is nonnegotiable.

Did we mention what a distinctive, idiosyncratic, eccentric, quirky, unconventional, and flat-out, out-of-the-ordinary place a baseball clubhouse is? Yup.

The problem is that Major League Baseball front offices often don't see it that way.

Making sure there were plenty of guardian-at-the-gate guys among the young talent—that was an understood piece of the puzzle, but it's been pushed to the back burner by a lot of executives. Too many executives.

More and more have been seduced by the idea of what might be. Let's not forget the proven commodities.

This evolution isn't difficult to decipher. What happened was that the technology revolution eased its way into the world of Major League Baseball, and the decision-makers took the bait. Prioritizing past performances and personalities slowly drifted away, with the siren call of potential winning out more and more.

Is he a good guy? Is he a good teammate? Will he be a solid mentor? No matter. His spin rate suggests that if we just alter the grip slightly on that two-seamer, all those failures will turn into a feather in our cap. Welcome to the new world of team-building.

There has to be a balance. There have to be those clubhouse-glue guys. The season is too long. The proximity of the lockers is too close. And the upbringings are two different. Fortunately, there can be both. I've lived it.

Look back at the early stages of that juggernaut of the Red Sox 2018 team, for instance. It was just a few weeks into the season when I plunked the Yankees' Tyler Austin, setting off a bench-clearing brawl between us and New York's "evil empire." At that time, we were rolling (winning nine straight after an Opening Day loss), with the image of me—fist cocked while hovering over a Yankee—seemingly only adding to the early-season electricity.

In some clubhouses, all would have been right with the world. Our leadership wouldn't let us buy into that mirage.

Throughout a baseball season, there are always boxes that need to be checked off, keeping things on the right track until the excitement of September and October takes over. And if those sorts of things go unchecked, then that's where problems can arise. That's why having the right voices in the clubhouse at the right time can often be twice as valuable as an extra few inches of break on somebody's slider.

In this case there was an issue about how some guys reacted to the middle-of-the-field melee. We knew we had a great bunch of guys—the right bunch of guys. But sometimes it's worth simply defining what is expected when such opportunities arise, and what was expected in this case was a bit more gumption to defend our own.

We could have that conversation because we had the voices to do so. Want to find the failings of any talented team? Start with the lack of leaders.

The fact that we won 108 regular season games and the World Series was no coincidence. And neither was our 2020 Dodgers club claiming that season's championship. You start with talent and then you make sure all corners of the clubhouse are accounted for.

There are boatloads of examples when not prioritizing the proper clubhouse dynamic made a team go sideways. One that jumps to mind is what I heard happened with the 2014 Seattle Mariners.

When July 6 rolled around, the Mariners were firmly in the postseason hunt, eight games over .500 and in position for the

Wild Card. Then the team decided John Buck—a veteran backup catcher who was hitting just about forty points under the league average—had to go. So, off he went. No big deal, right? Wrong.

Everyone in that clubhouse knew the importance of Buck's personality and leadership to that team, leading half the players to head into manager Lloyd McClendon's office to voice their displeasure. And, you know what? It turns out the players knew what was what.

The next month saw the Mariners' momentum drift away, going 9–14 while trying to find their post–John Buck identity. They would finish one game out of making the playoffs that year. Lesson learned (one would hope).

Like so many other things in baseball, teams are slowly coming back around to at least a portion of what previously worked before—clubhouse chemistry—and understanding the extremes of analytics aren't necessarily the gold mine they once thought.

Baseball might be the most unique game of them all. Cookie cutters don't work in this world. Just ask anybody who has lived that clubhouse life. Just ask the guy from Corona, California, who wanted to become an undercover agent.

Then there is the payoff.

I can explain what it's like to be a good teammate, how to navigate a major league clubhouse and make it through a big-league season. But what is virtually impossible to explain is when all these rivers converge into that final out of a championship season. Accurately describing what it feels like to go through it all and ultimately celebrate as a champion is simply impossible.

Go look at the faces of those players hoisting any championship trophy, or the childlike euphoria exhibited during title-induced celebrations. That's a good start when attempting to unearth that feeling. Still, unless you have lived that life, it's a sensation that can't be defined.

You think you have an idea, and then it happens and you quickly realize you had no clue.

And the great thing about winning a baseball championship is that, when the ultimate goal is achieved, you find yourself spraying champagne and pouring beer on one another's heads in the very same clubhouses where the championship stew was cooked. All these ingredients thrown together, stirring for eight months and then hoping you had the right recipe.

Delicious.

The final course is always the bubbly. When you see those bottles of Monet lined up in the clubhouse after that final out, it sets something off. That's when it becomes real, which was why the first time I experienced it with the Cardinals, I wanted to let all the celebratory champagne seep into every bit of my body. One thing they don't tell you when preparing to become champions of Major League Baseball, however, is how much champagne stings your eyes.

Actor Anthony Mackie explained it best in a *Vanity Fair* article, saying, "The most painful thing, aside from sticking yourself with a needle, is getting champagne in your eyes." Fair. But in the same piece, tennis legend Roger Federer also added the most important part of the equation, succinctly explaining, "It's an awful feeling, but a good one at the same time."

Honest, I didn't care much that it hurt. You don't really worry about anything but sharing the experience with those teammates who came from all corners of the world, all dodging the same sort of baseball-induced trials and tribulations to uncover this remarkable end game.

People talk, but you don't hear them. There can be cool speeches, or speeches that are just white noise. It doesn't matter. Everything is trumped by the act of popping bottles. I don't remember them. I have photos on my phone just for the memories, but at the moment words don't matter much. Running around like a lunatic, spraying this concoction of French grapes is the reward.

There is another payoff that comes with these celebrations: Any remaining semblance of seniority goes out the window. If you're a rookie or a younger player, the first thing you do is find veterans who have been serving as taskmasters for the entire season and you get them. Players. Coaches. Even owners. This is the chance to drench the bane of your existence. It is unexpected punctuation to the already out-of-body experience.

It's like clockwork in these celebrations. After the rookies finish congregating with their crews, they spring out to ambush the veterans. This is their big chance. I did it. I went straight for guys like Chris Carpenter and Jake Westbrook, players who had given me all that tough love. This was the time I could lovingly say, "Fuck you!" right back. Then, of course, came the hug.

At that moment, there are no class designations. No service-time time cards. And nobody cares about birth certificates. One way or another, we have all been together, and now this is our very messy, very wet family portrait.

The Red Sox in 2018 was the best of the bunch. It was unbelievably cramped because of the diminutive size of that Dodger Stadium visitors' clubhouse, but that made it better. We had this laundry cart full of ice and beer that everybody jumped in like some sort of baptismal. Everybody was in that thing.

Two years later with the Dodgers, it just wasn't the same. Thanks, COVID. No popped bottles, nothing. It was terrible.

Justin Turner had tested positive during the game so our post-game celebration was made up of MLB ushering all of us, and our families, to go get tested for COVID immediately. At least we had the on-field party after that final pitch, which we demanded Turner be a part of despite his diagnosis. As sappy as it might sound, COVID regulations weren't going to break our brotherhood.

No matter. A championship is a championship, and a clubhouse is a clubhouse. And a championship clubhouse? That is a complicated concoction that ultimately offers an unmatched reward. Just like baseball.

CHAPTER FOUR

THE BULLPEN: DEALING WITH THE DOWNTIME

Sometimes we take for granted just how unique baseball is. While we're focusing on time of game, pace of play, and trying to keep up with its lightning-quick sports world brethren, there are elements of baseball that simply can't be found in any other athletic walk of life.

And within those proprietary pieces reside some of the best stories. They are the jumping-off points for our appreciation.

At the top of my list? The bullpen.

Understand that there is nothing like a baseball bullpen—a section of the ballpark where a good chunk of the team playing in the game is sent to be separate from the rest of the world. In other sports, benchwarmers are still required to sit in the middle of those actively participating. Special teams in football? Try having them not be glued to the shoulders of those running on and off the field. Nope. Baseball has cornered the market on this bizarre in-game existence, and I think it's another example why, in baseball, sitting around isn't always a bad thing.

How and why this area where baseball teams send their relief pitchers to ride out nine innings ever became a thing is a bit hazy. Some suggest it was originally a place for overflow crowds in the late 1800s, while others say the term "bullpen" was born from a brand of tobacco. Former manager Casey Stengel once suggested such a place existed because the other players in the dugout got sick of listening to pitchers waiting to go in "shooting the bull," forcing the team to jettison the gabby relievers to the far reaches of the park.

Whatever the case, all I know is that this place is a microcosm of the intricacies of baseball. You might think sitting and wait-ing can't work in this day and age of attention-span-challenged sports fans, but you have no idea.

You know the phrase, "You can't just flip a switch"? That's such bullshit. Tell that to the baseball fans who spill popcorn all over themselves jumping up to watch a 450-foot home run after spending the previous five pitches fending off foul balls while talking about the problems at work. Or, better yet, try telling that to a relief pitcher.

What's that? We just gave up a home run? Put a pin in that conversation about Taco Bell vs. Del Taco. See you later: I have to get major league hitters out. Just give me a handful of warm-up pitches—maybe three curves and a pair of changeups—remind me of the situation, and let's bring on the cannon fire.

Don't tell me, "You can't just show up and beat them." Sorry. Watch me show up and kick their ass.

Isn't appreciating the immediacy of the unknown a big part of what makes the truest baseball fans? It's also what separates the breed of ballplayers who are told to sit hundreds of feet away from their teammates in something called a bullpen.

Our reality—for both players and fans alike—is that ours is a game that feels too long. You have to check in and check out, while enjoying all kinds of moments in between. And bullpen guys are the best at realizing that.

In this game of waiting, waiting, waiting, and, suddenly, "Boom!" we are the poster boys for baseball's sometimes-uneven rhythms.

Another great thing about this dynamic is that—much like the rest of the baseball world—while there are general dimensions and parameters, that doesn't prevent the places and players from offering their own personality. Some bullpens are outside. Some are inside. Some have air-conditioning. Some are hot as hell. Some are made for fan interaction. Some live in under-the-stands isolation.

And then there are the inhabitants. You have shit-talkers. You have pranksters. You have introverts. You have people riddled with anxiety. You have fellas who want to talk about dinner plans. You have players who can't fathom thinking about anything other than if and when they will actually play in the game unfolding in front of them.

If there is a common thread for most relievers, it is that they aren't quite themselves until that spot in the game when they would typically pitch has come and gone. Panic. Panic. Panic. *Oh, I'm not going in. Too bad, I felt really good today.* That's not me. Just tell me when to pitch, I will stop whatever I'm doing and pitch. But I get it. Insecurities are part of human nature.

For me, what feels natural is having some sort of human interaction.

Fortunately, that's exactly what most baseball bullpens are built for. Believe me, I have plenty of examples to support such a theory.

For the most part, the world is ours—just a couple of coaches, bullpen catchers, and seven or so relief pitchers. We sit, and we talk, and we sit, and we talk. In 2018 with the Red Sox, we started a game where a cup was put on the right field wall in front of us, serving as a target for flicked sunflower seeds. We weren't competing in the baseball game, so we had to compete in something. By season's end I had 480 documented on-target seeds, with the runner-up coming in at 190. I took the game to the Dodgers and I dominated there as well.

(I have come to learn that bragging rights in a baseball season—even involving something that has nothing to do with the actual game—can go a long way.)

But the real memories come when our little community is infiltrated.

I remember one time in Philadelphia, where the fans are right on top of the visitors' bullpen, and one guy was all over one of my teammates, Heath Hembree. Heater, as we called him, is a great guy with a real dry sense of humor, but hardly possessed the kind of personality that is going to fire back at hecklers.

"Hey, Hembree. You only have a few thousand followers on Instagram. My sister has more than you. You're not cool." This guy was just relentless on Heater with that sort of stuff. Well, I look up and see this guy was wearing these really baggy basketball shorts, and anybody down below him could see right up into him. One look at this wardrobe and I knew exactly what I was going to do if he kept badgering Heath.

Sure enough, Heater walks out to stretch and here comes that guy again. "Hey, Hembree. You're so skinny-fat, your body looks like mashed potatoes!"

I immediately pop out and yell up, with an entire collection of fans hovering. "Shut the fuck up! You're body-shaming my friend? Guess what, we can all see up your shorts right now and everybody can see you have a real problem down below!"

You could not only hear the collective gasp in the stands, but it was impossible not to notice the girl this guy was with bursting out in laughter. Everyone in our bullpen started losing it, with mild-mannered Hembree even mustering up a "Yes, small wiener!" toward the heckler, whose reaction was just as classic as the insult itself, literally running away in shame.

Sometimes fans have to be reminded that we do have the ability to listen and speak, even while wearing a big-league uniform. One thing I have come to realize is that those wake-up calls come in all different forms and levels of intensity.

There was no better example of fan passion morphing into bullpen back-and-forth than what happened less than a month after my fracas with the Yankees' Tyler Austin and the memorable bench-clearing fray.

The Red Sox and Yankees rivalry is always hot—at least between the fan bases—so throw in an actual fight between the teams and that's only going to amp up the intensity. Sure, the fight had put me on the shoulders of New England baseball fans—as the sea of "Joe Kelly Fight Club" T-shirts suggests. But for Yankees fans, all it did was circle the day when I'd be in their crosshairs. That day was the eighth of May 2018, during our first trip to Yankee Stadium that season.

It should be noted that I love the Yankee Stadium bullpen. First off, it has actual climate control, which is key considering how much I hate the heat. And once you walk out to where the mounds are, there is the kind of energy and animosity that we should be celebrating throughout baseball. And, thanks to the Austin incident, I got a healthy dose of all the hate.

When Alex Cora called down to have me warm up in the seventh inning with the game tied, I wasn't surprised. After being the least popular player on the 2018 Red Sox for the first two weeks of the season thanks to an Opening Day implosion, I had reversed course, both in the eyes of my manager and the fans. We had gone on an absolute tear after the fight, and I hadn't given up a run in my next nine outings, striking out twelve in 9 2/3 innings. By the time that call came down to the bullpen in the Bronx, we were all feeling pretty good about ourselves.

During that whole game, the fans out by the bullpen were in rare form, raining insults and objects down on our area. And we're not talking about paper airplanes here. People were spending $12 on a beer just to throw it at us. It was all part of the deal.

So, when I walked out to warm up, snatching the ball from our bullpen coach, Craig Bjornson, I briefly looked up behind him. There were all these gang-looking guys glaring down. All the tattoos and trademarks I had come to know while fending off these sorts of dudes in Southern California.

"Hey, pussy!" one of them yelled.

I stopped my throwing and shot back, "What's up, motherfucker?"

"Hey, we're going to fucking kill you!" he shot back, making a threatening motion with his hand.

"Oooh. Nice finger gun," I responded, at which point a cop started drifting down toward the situation. "Hey, that guy just threatened my life. Are you going to do something or are you a Yankees fan, too?" I asked the officer.

I turned my attention back to my new friends, telling them exactly where the team bus would be and when they could meet me. Suddenly, it felt like the entire stadium had descended down on our little corner of the world to join these gang guys. This was not going to let up any time soon. Finally, my number was called, and I headed out to face Aaron Judge with the bases loaded. By then the air was so unbelievably thick with animosity, I felt launched out of the bullpen doors. What can oftentimes be the longest of jogs from the far reaches of where we warm up to the actual pitching mound seemed like one of the best times of my professional life.

This is what baseball is all about.

I have been part of games where the fans seemed to take over, including the 2012 Wild Card game when the umpires took away a Braves rally by calling an infield fly rule, helping our Cardinals win that game. But until this game, the jeers had never been so laser-focused in my direction. For an adrenaline junkie like myself, this was the ultimate fix. And, ironically, ever since that night, that Yankee Stadium bullpen has been one of my favorites. The gang guys never came back, but plenty of their Yankee-loving friends certainly have. And, believe it or not, not all of them hate me, probably because they realize passion and personality are part of the lifeblood of our game.

And it doesn't have to be all about anger and animosity. Our bullpen world is out among those fans who—like us—are sitting hundreds of feet away from the game's main characters. We can help with something baseball does better than any other sport: make memories.

The bullpens at Fenway, Yankee Stadium, and Dodger Stadium are great because they give us relievers the perspective of the fans. The true fans. Nobody out by the bullpen is part of a corporate package or carries the cache of a season-ticket holder. These are the folks who view the baseball-watching experience for what it should be—a meticulous, multilayered, good-time meeting among friends.

So, when a kid starts yelling down to play "Rock, Paper, Scissors," I'm not going to turn my back and find an excuse not to. Let's play some "Rock, Paper, Scissors"! When the cameras caught me going back and forth with a young fan, that wasn't the first or last time. In that case, we were playing two out of three, with a baseball being the payoff if he won. He didn't win. No ball. Life lessons. But you know what? A few weeks later some kid in Kansas City smoked me. He got the baseball.

There has to be this back-and-forth between players and the fans. We're all in this big, beautiful world of baseball together. Whether it is through silly kid games, or military men dropping down some sand from Iwo Jima for me, or the art of the trade— such as a game jersey for a mariachi jacket.

My best trade started with a simple game of catch between me and Kenley Jansen back in 2021 at Dodger Stadium. I was doing what I always do, throwing the baseball and surveying those taking the time to watch me. There are always subtle differences in the crowd gathering around to watch big leaguers get ready for these games, but this one time there was a pack of observers who had jumped out in a not-so-subtle way.

There they were. Mariachi musicians.

For me, the sight of the Mexican music-makers scratched right where I itched, because of my love for the genre and the idea that they would be integrated into this sometimes-sterile baseball-playing environment. I had no idea that some believe "mariachi" is derived from the French word for marriage, *marriage*, but it sure seemed apropos. In my mind, these guys and the

Major League Baseball crowd I yearned for were a perfect fit. Baseball needed more mariachi bands.

"Hey, play your instruments," I yelled up to them from the bullpen. Soon my teammate Kenley Jansen jumped in to double-down on the request. "Yeah, play your instruments!"

"We don't have them," one of the group members yelled down.

"Well, go get them," I shot back.

So off they went and five minutes later they were playing away up in the bleachers. Not good enough. "Play them down here," Kenley shouted. We needed a soundtrack while we warmed up, and these guys had presented the perfect opportunity for just that. So, after some conversations with security, down they came, playing away right behind us while we threw our baseballs.

My interest didn't stop there.

"Hey, those jackets are sick," I told one of the guys. "How about if I trade one of my jerseys for a jacket?"

"Oh, man, I can't. This is my uniform. We have to perform tonight," he said.

In my mind, of all the gifts lowered down by fans, this was going to be the pièce de résistance. "Maybe after?" I countered.

"Maybe," he said, going off to make his mariachi magic happen for an audience larger than just me and Kenley.

Well, the game comes and goes, leaving me sort of bummed out while sitting in the bullpen. My potential trade partner never reappeared.

Then, the next day in the third inning, I hear somebody yelling at me. It's the mariachi guy and his girlfriend shouting down into the bullpen, "Hey! You want the jacket?"

"What?"

"It's me. The mariachi guy from yesterday."

"Oh, shit. It is!"

So, there he was, holding my new favorite jacket high in the air. "I'll trade you," he yelled. "I came back. I said I would trade you."

Hell, yeah!

Immediately, I ran into the clubhouse and told the guys in there that I needed that jersey I'd planned on trading the day before. They dug it up, I ran back out, and I breathlessly screamed, "I got it!" So down came the mariachi jacket and up went number 17. My first official bullpen trade with a fan was complete.

"Look, boys," I said a few minutes later, walking back into the clubhouse to show whomever was there my new prized possession. "I got the jacket." A cheer went up. My day had been brightened—and my wardrobe was made exponentially more extravagant—all thanks to baseball and one of its many fun-loving followers.

It was a reminder of the importance of this relationship that we as players have to nurture.

Sometimes it's easy to forget why these fans are spending their hard-earned money to watch us play baseball. As players, we sit there in the bullpen, waiting, watching, and talking. But, for us, at least there is an actual chance to pick up a baseball and start throwing it. The closest those sitting in the seats will come to an experience with a piece of equipment is if a ball happens to be hit somewhere in their direction. (I get the desperation and intent people have when it comes to securing any foul ball or home run. This is their opportunity to actually touch the portrait that is being painted for three-plus hours.)

Once the paychecks start coming, the opportunities for these reminders go out the window.

It's why, when I was presented with a few games off, thanks to the kerfuffle with the Yankees, I was going to make the most of the opportunity. I was going to sit in the stands to live a life I had left behind long ago—that of an actual fan.

The first stop was the Fenway Park bleachers. After going through all the pregame stuff with my teammates—stretching, lifting, treatment, throwing—I took off my uniform, left the clubhouse, and started serving the suspension handed down from Major League Baseball. I could have gone home. But why would I want to do that when I could get the perspective of those actually paying to be at the ballpark? It was time to remember why people cheered, booed, stuck around until the eighth inning to sing "Sweet Caroline," and came back to do it all over again.

So, in about the third inning, I walked up to my seat—planting myself eleven rows in back of my bullpen brethren. It was just about fifty feet from where my usual perch was, but it felt like a world away. In the blink of an eye, I had lost my identity as a Major League Baseball player. I kind of liked it.

A little while later, I moved my seats to a couple different places in the park, ending in a suite, where Patriots wide receiver Julian Edelman was also taking in the game. While that is admittedly a completely different existence than the sun-soaked life in back of the bullpen, the feeling was the same. I imagined this was what it felt like to be retired. It was a glimpse into why some former players don't come back. It's a tease. You are at the game, but not in the game.

What I found out is that as difficult as it was to zero in as a relief pitcher relegated to the bullpen, living the life as a fan can be a completely different deal. You are far away. People around you are hammered. The thirst for action has as much to do with socializing as it does waiting for the big hit. It was definitely different from life as one of the participants, but sometimes different isn't all that bad. At least that was the case on the final day of my suspension.

The Fenway experience was the capper for my foray into the world of fandom. While we were in Toronto—marking day one of my suspension—I told the guys I was going to find the highest seat in Rogers Centre. But I also knew any true fan wore the jersey of one of their favorite players if possible. Fortunately, one of my favorites—Hembree—was more than willing to lend me his blue game jersey for the game. So, up I went. After a lengthy elevator ride and what seemed like a billion steps, I found my spot, not too far off from the top of the left-field foul pole. My goal was to find the worst seat in the place. Mission accomplished.

Beer and pretzel in hand, I delivered on my promise to my teammates that I would confirm my safe arrival. On went the light on my phone, raising it high in the air like a one-spectator concert. I could barely make out the small images of my teammates trickling out of the dugout to witness the payoff on my promise—some were waving for me to come down with snacks in hand.

I couldn't help but think about what watching a baseball game from that vantage point would be like. My conclusion was that, whether it was up in those nosebleeds or from the angle of a reliever waiting for his turn to pitch, much of this ballpark life is about the experience. Friends. Food. Family.

Another thing that hits home is this: The process of navigating the length of a baseball game continues to evolve—not only for the fans, but for those groups of players who have been sent to sit among them, the relief pitchers.

The isolated few. Those who are on the team, but not really.

We can talk about the games we play while in the bullpen, the conversations with one another and occasionally with the folks in the stands. But what can't be forgotten is how baseball now views our existence as baseball players.

It used to be so simple. You hope a starting pitcher can pitch six, seven, or eight innings, getting teams to two or three relievers designated as the prelude to the be-all, end-all, hair-on-fire closer. There were a few other guys down there, of course, serving as break-glass-in-case-of-emergency long relievers. Those were the ones who weren't good enough to start, but also couldn't be relied on consistently to get one inning's worth of outs when it counted the most.

Everybody knew exactly when they were going to pitch, and that's how it was, whether they liked it or not. In other words, the set-up men and closers could basically take a nap until the seventh inning.

Now? Daydreaming isn't an option anymore.

In 2021, there wasn't a single relief pitcher with as many as forty saves, and just nine totaled thirty or more. Ten years prior, eight relievers had forty or more saves, with nineteen managing at least thirty.

This has become all about pockets, those spots in the lineup the manager believes his pitcher's skill set outmatches specific hitters. Forget about the image of the closer, whose sole responsibility used to be to secure the final three outs. Sure, some of those guys exist, but in the eyes of executives, they are no more important than the four, five, or even six pitchers coming in before them.

In my last year with the Dodgers, the one spot in the batting order I faced the least was the No. 9 hitter. That was no coincidence.

Where is this leading us? To a conversation that involves more than just us relievers.

Starting pitchers used to be the be-all, end-all. They got paid the most, leaving a lot of relievers pining to become one of them. I lived the life. Believe me, when I was moved to the bullpen in 2016 after starting my whole professional career, I could feel the dollars flying out of my bank account. We were, after all, raised on the idea that a mediocre starting pitcher made just about the same as the best relievers. But now? The value of a starter for a lot of teams just isn't what it used to be, considering that pitching for five innings is now cause for celebration.

To be honest, the winners of this phenomenon are pitchers like me. I'm the guy who is going to allow you not to push your starter a third time through the batting order, swooping in to face the meat-and-potatoes lineup when it counts the most. Wins. Saves. Even ERA. None of it will define my worth. But the front offices will open the checkbook a bit more for guys of my ilk.

Will we be getting the money befitting all those aces and closers of yesteryear? Nope. But at least the talents of those previously viewed as not-ready-for-prime-time players are being rewarded with a previously unheard of financial pat on the back.

I do have to admit, however, the whole shift is not good for marketing baseball. There is something to be said for the next generation of baseball fans viewing both starting pitchers and closers as godlike figures. When you knew which game you were going to, the first thing to do was count the days and decipher exactly which starting pitcher was going to highlight your experience.

"I've got the Clayton Kershaw ticket!" That used to be a thing. Well, you better soak in that starter as much as possible for those first few innings, because the final third of your baseball-viewing experience is going to be all about getting to know a bunch of relief pitchers.

In 2021, there were seven teams with as many as three complete games. Once again, going back ten years, twenty-three clubs managed at least three. You get the idea.

The next question is, can this actually work?

It depends.

You have to understand that baseball players—above most human beings—are creatures of habit. They show up in the clubhouse at a certain time. They get dressed a certain way. They eat a certain food. They travel a certain way. And they definitely like to know with some certainty when to get ready for their big moments. That's what makes this new way of doing things a little tricky.

About twenty years ago, Boston general manager Theo Epstein tried rolling out something similar to this flexible bullpen use, with the 2003 Red Sox entering that season with something someone decided to call "Bullpen by Committee." Instead of a few designated stud closers being relied on to shut the door, Epstein was going to have his team bob and weave its way through a lineup using five or six candidates.

Well, it didn't work out all that well, and by May the Red Sox were relying on traditional closers the rest of the way. Despite the failed experiment, Epstein was quoted midway through that season as saying, "Ten years from now, everybody is going to be doing it." He was definitely on to something.

As we have come to discover, such a blueprint can work, but there are two must-haves that the Red Sox team probably didn't possess. First, you must have pitchers good enough to pull it off. Second—and this is where I have seen the approach made or broken—there must be next-level communication. The Dodgers and our manager there, Dave Roberts, got that. They were best at making sure no stone was unturned when it came to figuring out how each reliever was going to find his optimum moment in the sun.

Every single game was scripted. We knew exactly what day we were going to pitch and who we were going to face. There was very little room for interpretation. Nobody on base. Three, four, and five hitters coming up. You're in. It didn't matter the inning. No closer title needed. That was that.

It's like any job. Guys have to feel comfortable. The information. The roles. The communication. All of it took away the anxiety.

In the words of Australian novelist Morris West, "If you spend your whole life waiting for the storm, you'll never enjoy the sunshine."

Welcome to the bullpen. Welcome to baseball.

CHAPTER FIVE

GIVING BASEBALL THE BUSINESS

I'm not a big inspirational quotation guy. It's not like I stare up at the placards these teams like to put on doors, walls, and windows for baseball players to soak in while coming around every single corner. The reminders are well intentioned, for sure.

But every once in a while you come across a few words uttered by someone at some time in some place that make you stop and think. One of those just so happened to be passed on by a guy making his mark on the other side of Chicago.

His name was Phil Wrigley. (If that sounds familiar, it should. He has a pretty well-known ballpark named after his family.) These were the words he relayed that surprisingly stuck in my brain:

Baseball is too much of a sport to be a business and too much of a business to be a sport.

Amen.

I started looking into this guy who gave us this saying, and I learned he was a businessman who had inherited a gum company and baseball team, the Cubs, from his father. But he also clearly cared about the game while managing the moneymaking side of things. When World War II threatened to derail baseball, he was the guy who kept baseball on the brain in this country, sponsoring the All-American Girls Professional Baseball League. (The story is retold in the movie *A League of Their Own*.) Wrigley prioritized the kind of media coverage for the Cubs—both in print and electronically—that would make sure the Wrigley stands remained full, even when there were no baseball playoffs.

It seemed like Mr. Wrigley had a good grasp of the unavoidable two sides of our game. Or at least he attempted to understand it. I can't say that for most of the current owners.

The challenge that Wrigley wrestled with started when baseball officially became a business in the 1860s and it hasn't died down since. But it's clear some try to tackle the dichotomy more than others, with too few seeming to care all that much about the actual joy of the game.

For me, this isn't about labor negotiations or the like. This is about actually loving all that baseball brings, and exhibiting some of that adulation along the way. Compared to other sports, our owners' safe haven is the boardroom rather than the ball fields. And that's sad.

With the understanding that one has to be really, really wealthy to own a Major League Baseball team, it's time to prioritize getting some younger, more enthusiastic bodies in those owners' chairs. Elon Musk. Mark Cuban. Mark Zuckerberg. Let's go! We see the Steve Ballmers of the world sit courtside for his Los Angeles Clippers, living and dying with every play. I'm sure there are some in our baseball-ownership world who might secretly yearn to portray a similar image, but it certainly is hard to find them.

And it's not just about the fist pumps or social media engagement. This is also about prioritizing ideas that will actually draw people to baseball instead of stiff-arming them with talks of bottom lines and luxury tax thresholds. These are smart people who probably got to where they are by seeing through a prism others weren't aware of. Now is the time to start utilizing that sort of vision for the game they are supposed to be reveling in.

Call me naïve, but I want owners arguing with umpires, pouring celebratory beer down their gullets, and then eating a post-game ice cream with their buddies to revel in what they just saw. And then, to top it off, go back to their offices and figure out algorithms that help enable some better fan-friendly apps.

I'm not arguing that there isn't a balancing act when it comes to the separation between the business side of baseball and appeasing the ball and bat crowd. But there has to be better recognition by both the check-signers and the suits in Major League Baseball that this is a partnership.

Believe me, there have been plenty of times since I entered this world of professional baseball that it felt like the suits and I were living in completely different worlds. Some really, really uncomfortable times. One, in particular, jumps to mind.

Remember the pitch to Bregman, the words with Correa, and finally the pout? Well, evidently, all of it served as the biggest reality check when it came to how quickly our game can devolve into us—the players—versus them—the guys at 1271 6th Avenue in New York City (otherwise known as the commissioner's office).

For me, one of the greatest sins in our professional lives is the abuse of faith and trust, with the abuse of power not far behind.

Thanks to the fallout from that day in Houston, all of it was put on display at my expense.

While there are hundreds of big and small decisions passed down from the offices in Manhattan every year, portraying the good and bad of whatever process big business baseball has decided to set up, I can only give you my hallmark moment, one that painted the kind of picture that makes those words from Mr. Wrigley ring through my head.

Let me take you inside the wonderful world of a Major League Baseball suspension:

Starting with a letter . . .

> Major League Baseball
> 1271 Avenue of the Americas
> New York, NY 10020
> July 29, 2020

Mr. Joe Kelly
Los Angeles Dodgers
1000 Vin Scully Avenue
Los Angeles, CA 90012

Dear Joe,

I have read the Umpire Incident Report filed by Crew Chief Alfonso Marquez and reviewed the video of the Los Angeles Dodgers–Houston Astros game on July 28, 2020.

During the bottom of the sixth inning of that game, you violated Official Baseball Rule 6.02(c)(9) by intentionally throwing your fourth pitch of the at-bat in the head area of Astros batter Alex Bregman. The comment to Official

Baseball Rule 6.02(c)(9) states, in part, that, "[t]o pitch at a batter's head is unsportsmanlike and highly dangerous. It should be and is condemned by everybody." In addition, after later striking out Carlos Correa to end the inning, you taunted Correa and directed comments and gestures toward the Astros dugout as you walked off the mound. Your actions directly contributed to the ensuing bench-clearing incident. While this behavior is unacceptable during any season, it is especially egregious when viewed in the context of the 2020 season, when any actions that can lead to close contact between players and coaches or prolong a game can have particularly stark consequences. In the future, I implore you to be more mindful of your actions, particularly given the risks to all involved in this season.

Your actions on the field were dangerous and offensive, and showed a reckless disregard for the safety and well-being of the players on both Clubs. Your actions and comments did not conform to the high standards of personal conduct and good sportsmanship required of you as a Major League Player. Accordingly, you are hereby suspended for eight (8) games and fined $10,000.00. Your suspension is scheduled to begin during your Club's game tonight on July 29, 2020.

During the course of your suspension, you may be in uniform and may participate in your regular pre-game routine. At game time, however, you must be out of uniform and away from team areas. You are permitted to watch the game from the suite level, but may not at any time be in the dugout, bullpen, press box or any broadcast areas.

Your personal check in the amount of $10,000.00 (made payable to either the Baseball Assistance Team or the MLB-MLBPA Youth Development Foundation) should be

sent to the Department of On-Field Operations at Major
League Baseball (attention: Danielle Monday) by Friday,
August 7, 2020.

Respectfully,
Chris Young, SVP, On-Field Operations
cc: LAD—Baseball Operations; MLB—On-Field
Operations, Labor Relations; Bob Lenaghan (MLBPA)

Now, let's view the aforementioned umpire's report:

Umpire Incident Report
Major League Baseball
245 Park Avenue
New York, NY 10167

Reporting Umpire: Marquez, Alfonso
Submitted: 07/29/2020
Published: 07/29/2020

UMPIRE DEPARTMENT COMMENTS

*LAD pitcher Kelly intentionally threw a pitch behind HOU batter
Bregman. No action was taken by the Umpire Crew. Comments and
gestures were exchanged at various points during the inning. During
HOU batter Correa's at-bat, Kelly threw a breaking pitch that forced
Correa to duck out of the way. The pitch was not deemed intentional by
the Umpire Crew and no action was taken. Correa struck out to end the
inning and words and gestures were exchanged between Kelly and
Correa and other Astros. The benches cleared onto the field as this*

*exchange escalated. Warnings were issued to both Clubs prior to the
game resuming.*

GAME INFORMATION

HP: Marquez   1B: Guccione   2B: Blaser   3B: Morales
LAD @ HOU 07/28/2020 08:11 PM ET

GAME SITUATION 1

LAD—5 HOU-2   TOP—7TH
BALLS—0   STRIKES—0   OUTS—0

ROBERTS, DAVE
Warning
Warnings issued to prevent retaliation (pitch not involved
in incident)
W1

BAKER JR., DUSTY
Warning
Warnings issued to prevent retaliation (pitch not involved
in incident)
W1

KELLY, JOE
Warning
Other comments and gestures
W1

CORREA, CARLOS
Warning
Other comments and gestures
W1

How long did this incident delay the game? 5 Mins.
Was a "Heads-Up" in place for this game? No
Was the incident reported by telephone following the
    game? Yes

INCIDENT DESCRIPTION

During the bottom of the sixth inning, Alex Bregman was
up to bat for the Houston Astros with one out, no runners
on base.

UMPIRE INCIDENT REPORT

Major League Baseball
245 Park Avenue

A 3–0 count. Joe Kelly was pitching for the Dodgers. The
3–0 pitch to Bregman went over and behind his head. I
deemed this pitch to be intentionally thrown behind him.
There was a little bit of chatter from the Houston dugout.
Pitcher Kelly then threw over to first base three consecutive
times and Houston's dugout would say something after every
time but nothing that would make us say something or get
together. Later on in the inning, Carlos Correa was up to
bat with a runner on first and two outs. The first pitch to
Correa was an off speed pitch that went over Correa's head.

I did not deem this pitch intentional and nothing was said by anyone. Correa ended up striking out to end the inning.

AFTER EFFECTS: After Correa struck out, Dodgers' pitcher Kelly looked toward Houston's dugout and that's when Houston started yelling out at Kelly. Kelly continued toward his dugout while making facial expressions at Houston. By now both teams started out of their dugouts and onto the field. Our crew got in the middle of both teams and were telling them to go back. Only words were exchanged. Once we got everybody back to their dugouts we got together and decided to issue warnings to both teams. I informed Dodgers' Manager Dave Roberts and Chris Guccione informed Astros' Manager Dusty Baker. Baker immediately came out of the dugout telling us that they did nothing to be warned. We told Baker that warnings were in and that it needed to be the end of it. Manager Baker then went back to the dugout and we continued and ended the game with no further incidents.

THIS REPORT HAS BEEN REVIEWED AND APPROVED FOR TRANSMISSION BY THE CREW CHIEF.

• • •

So, there you have it. They suspended me for eight games and fined me $10,000 for throwing a pitch near Bregman's head and then making a funny face. OK, then.

So much is great about being a big-league ballplayer, but one thing I have found to be the opposite of excellent is having to listen to a bunch of MLB executives tie themselves into knots suggesting that I almost caused a COVID-super-spreader brawl. And while I sat through this back-and-forth, I knew that there was an ulterior motive at play.

In the eyes of Major League Baseball, two things needed to be painted in a positive light at that place and time: Its protection of the cheating Astros and how it was handling the COVID chaos.

Other than a player's approach to throwing or hitting or running on a baseball field, one of the most important decisions he can make is picking the right people to shield him from the big, bad world of baseball business. Fortunately, I had chosen Sam and Seth Levinson of an agency called ACES (Athletes' Careers Enhanced and Secured Inc.).

What you notice immediately about the brothers is that, while they are diminutive in size, their presence is huge.

Intensity. Information. Opinion. They are all offered up with every conversation I have had with those guys. You can tell how much they care and how much they have worked to get to this level of sports agency prestige. Two smart kids from Brooklyn who simply loved the game of baseball so much that they dedicated their lives to helping guys like me navigate the roads we players really have no desire to venture down.

Sam and Seth care. And that was never more evident than when trying to fend off the warped world of Major League Baseball decision-makers.

In this case, Seth, who is an attorney, had five minutes—five minutes!—to right what we believed to be wrong: suspending me for no legitimate reason. I sat. I listened. And I couldn't believe how those from Major League Baseball were representing the situation, while simply turning a blind eye to the facts before them. They were so dug in on their agenda—protecting the perceived safety of the cheating Astros while showing that MLB was preventing players from spreading COVID—that the facts bounced off their heads. At least, that's how it seemed from where I was sitting.

Those days of worrying about how to wear my uniform seemed so far away.

Did I mention in this hearing that they let my agent speak for exactly five minutes? Five minutes! But, you know what? Seth sure squeezed a lot in those three hundred seconds. Later, my agent—a veteran of hundreds of such cases—said he hadn't seen anything like it. Neither had I.

The first thing he reminded the group was that I was "charged" with "intentionally" throwing at Bregman's head. Chris Young, who was the disciplinary czar for MLB, had issued an over-the-top statement about the seriousness of throwing at a player's head, reading like an indictment. The beauty of it was that Seth actually got everyone to agree that such an action must be treated as a serious crime. In fact, it was the most serious crime that can be committed by a pitcher.

So far, so good.

Where MLB's case all started going to crap was when Seth pointed out that the word "head" appeared nowhere in the umpire's report. The omission of "head" in the umpire's report, under those circumstances, was like charging someone with murder even though none of the police reports mentioned murder.

When asked to describe the offense, the umpire's report refers to the offense as "routine." You would have thought that throwing at someone's head would be anything but routine. Of course, the conclusion that the offense was routine supported the umpire's decision not to eject me.

Notably, MLB had sent a memo before the 2020 season instructing umpires to confer over any pitch that may be intentional to determine whether or not an ejection is warranted. Well, the umpires didn't confer, which meant it was evident to the four umpires that my pitch was not thrown intentionally at Bregman's head.

Now, the umpire's report does state that the pitch was thrown "intentionally behind the batter." Guess what? There is absolutely nothing in the *Official Rules of Major League Baseball* that prohibits a pitcher from throwing behind a hitter, which only underscored the conclusion that I didn't violate any rule or commit any offense that was deserving of a suspension.

And to top it all off, the MLB attorney wanted Seth's argument to be stricken from the record. That would have been an interesting approach . . . if there was actually a record being taken.

Reminder: No batter was hit by a pitch. There were no ejections. No warnings were issued before the pitch. And there was no fight after the pitch. Never, in the history of baseball, has there ever been a pitcher suspended without any of the aforementioned four events taking place.

What MLB was saying was that the pitch to Bregman was far too inside. (That was MLB, not the umpires.)

So, what we did was submit an exhibit that demonstrates that since 2018 there had been fifteen pitches thrown that were further inside than my offering to Bregman, and seven that were thrown as far inside without the pitcher being disciplined. In other words, the whole suspension was completely arbitrary.

My perspective on this charade was that every bit of evidence we threw at them was simply brushed aside, with their counterarguments based only on my character. For instance, when the benches cleared and the Astros confronted me just feet from the Dodgers' dugout, MLB Senior Counsel Justin Wiley accused me of putting the season at risk and jeopardizing the health and safety of the umpires because the chance that COVID would spread without social distancing had now increased. Huh?!

Here was what we desperately tried to explain to them: The pitch to Bregman was unintentional, I had been effectively wild throughout my career, and this pitch wasn't unlike so many others I had thrown throughout my career.

Hell, I threw seventeen pitches without throwing a single fastball for a strike, and I had only one pitch (a curveball) called for a strike. I walked two hitters on eight pitches, threw a wild pitch, and got Correa out by throwing six consecutive breaking balls. How could I intentionally throw a pitch at anyone that day, considering I had no idea where any of the pitches were going?

The next problem for MLB was a ridiculous exhibit they presented. It demonstrated that over the course of my career I had hit seventeen right-handed batters with fastballs. When asked about the fraudulent exhibit, Wiley held his ground and said it accurately reflected my fastball location to right-handed hitters in my career.

So, we decided to take it one step further to see how much of a joke this was going to be.

Seth and company duplicated the MLB exhibit by using its own Statcast data. This was *their* information. The result was hysterical, leading MLB to submit a revised exhibit after the hearing. (Who knew the parties could submit evidence after both parties had rested their cases?)

MLB decided to change the period measured for fastballs over my career to fastballs spanning 2015–2020. (It was curious that they chose such a specific time period.) And finally, they eliminated the image of the batter from the exhibit so that it didn't look so obvious that they were missing the seventeen right-handed batters I hit with fastballs.

Wiley then stated separately to the arbitrator that the exhibit was limited to only four-seam fastballs, when nowhere in the actual exhibit was the selection of pitches that specific. That was odd, considering the pitch I threw to Bregman was a two-seam fastball.

Ultimately this was the kind of kangaroo court that would have embarrassed a kangaroo. MLB had its narrative and its motivations, and it wasn't going to let facts get in the way.

I love playing in Major League Baseball. It's a dream come true. But, like a lot of things in life, reality isn't quite as pristine as those childhood fantasies might suggest.

My head-butting with MLB didn't stop with the hearing or latest suspension. The league put me at the top of the list when it came to fines for not wearing my mask during the shortened 2020 season. We're talking $1,000 a pop. But what was bizarre about those reports was that even though there was supposedly an official in the dugout and clubhouse assigned to monitor such things, they never approached me or presented a photo of my supposed transgressions.

Heck, one time they wrote me up for an incident in a game where I had pulled my mask down to drink water. *Sigh.*

All of this comes back to my biggest problem with MLB and, in some cases, the teams it oversees: the abuse of power. Can we please start doing the right thing without players having to push and push and push? Some of it is just flat-out common sense.

For instance, Major League Baseball has access to all of these Wall Street executives, so why in the world can't it set up a committee for players who are retired or about to be retired that can help them with investment information? The unfortunate fact is that 60 percent of MLB players who retire have financial problems.

Or how about this? Set up an independent committee involving mental health professionals who can really help a problem that is lingering among players these days. There needs to be somebody for these guys to talk to if they don't trust who the clubs are offering up, or if there is an issue that crops up in the middle of the night. Right now everything has to be done through the club, and that doesn't always work for a player.

There also can't be a paint-by-numbers approach when it comes to treatment for issues such as attention-deficit/hyperactivity disorder. I get it. Medication like Ritalin is a powerful supplement for baseball players. As one player said, it can make you immediately offer so much focus that you can make out what people are talking about in the upper deck. But some guys legitimately need it, and even if they go to a renowned psychiatrist, the disorder is diagnosed, and a prescription is written, MLB will not approve it. That doesn't seem right.

You have all of these instances piling up, and it's hard to not feel like MLB and its clubs are viewing the players more and more like property. Unfortunately it's a feeling that is becoming more prevalent by the day.

All that said, I do fully appreciate the financial opportunities that come with playing baseball in the major leagues for a living. How can you not? Built on the backs of those who came well before me, the world of baseball has afforded me the chance to live life like a millionaire. And I'm getting those paychecks because of an actual game. The best game. That isn't lost on me.

So, when my first foray into free agency came around, it was another level of surreal. Six years of service time in the big leagues had put me in the position to see if teams actually valued what I did. It turns out they did.

The feeling of being a free agent in baseball can be like college recruiting. It's nice to have interest from schools, but all of it is semi-white noise while waiting for that top choice to give a ring. Fortunately for me, after the 2019 season ended, that call came.

Thank goodness for the Dodgers.

I loved Boston for many reasons, including how they had helped define my existence heading into my first crack at free agency. After trading for me in 2014, the expectation from everyone involved was that my world would continue to be as a starter. I had done just enough to suggest there was promise, so that when I walked over to the guys at WEEI Sports Radio in Foxwoods during the offseason prior to 2015 and told listeners I was going to win the Cy Young (the award given each year to Major League Baseball's best pitchers), a case was actually being made.

Every pitcher wants to hold opponents to under a sub-.240 batting average and win a lot along the way. It has always been understood that if you do those two things as a starting pitcher, you're going to make more money than the equally-as-successful relievers. The biggest contracts almost always go to the starters. That's why relievers will gladly prioritize life as a starting pitcher if given the opportunity, and it's also the reason middle-of-the-road starters, like myself, usually bristle at the idea of heading into the bullpen.

I was no different . . . until I was.

The transformation from starter to reliever started in 2016 and truly took root in 2017, when I ended up pitching in fifty-four games with a 2.79 ERA. By the time the 2018 season rolled around, all the feels and adrenaline I had thrived on while performing as a relief pitcher in college had surged back. I came to love it. I loved how the mind worked in those big spots, prioritizing the here and the now instead of the long haul. And I felt like I was pretty good at it, especially in the postseason where I had given up a run just once in twelve playoff games.

It wasn't until the final weeks of the 2018 season when everything about my pitching truly changed. Dana LeVangie, the Red Sox pitching coach, finally pushed aside my final stumbling block. Grit. Guile. Stuff. Fearlessness. All welcome elements. But when LeVangie got me to understand that my curveball was my best weapon—not necessarily the much-talked-about 100 mph heater—it changed everything.

For such a sometimes-complicated game, it's amazing how often fortunes can be defined in baseball with simple bits of information.

The alteration wasn't really put on display until our postseason run, which culminated in the "Fuck, yeah!" moment in Game 6 of the World Series at Dodger Stadium. I had pitched in nine playoff games, allowing one earned run while striking out eleven and not walking a single batter. And it was all punctuated by those three strikeouts in the eighth inning.

I didn't realize it at the time, but the Dodgers had taken notice beyond just licking their wounds from that final night of the 2018 season. They saw the change I had made and were intrigued. As it turned out, very intrigued.

When free agency rolled around and I found out the Dodgers were interested, it was a game changer. You're talking about a ballpark I could drive to from my home, and a team that is actually going to play in important games. Then I met with Dodgers president Andrew Friedman, and there was no doubt which team had jumped to the top of the list.

For three hours we talked, with Friedman explaining in great detail how the Dodgers saw my evolution, where they wanted to build on it from there, and exactly how all of the future success was going to happen. There were analytics. There were machines. There were explanations of what was expected not only from the pitchers but also the catchers when it came to zeroing in on game plans.

After my visit with Friedman, in my mind, the Dodgers were the future. They were *my* future.

Decisions would be made at the upcoming Baseball Winter Meetings, the four-day event held every December and attended by representatives of all thirty Major League Baseball teams and the 120 minor league teams to discuss business, offseason trades, and so on.

There were other teams trying to do what the Dodgers were doing when it came to information and approach, but it sure seemed like Los Angeles was a few steps ahead of the rest of the pack. For me it was: This is the pitch you should throw, where you should throw it, when you should throw it, and here are the hitters you will be throwing it to. There were other layers of suggestions and observations; for example, they identified that my triple-digit fastball was getting hit so often because I was throwing it with one finger instead of two. To say all of it was eye-opening is an understatement.

And, did I mention, they played really close to my house?

So, that's why when I sat down for dinner on the last night of the Baseball Winter Meetings at my California home and got the message from Sam and Seth that it seemed like we might be getting our wish, I went to bed a happy camper. The guys told me to keep my ringer on, and they would be getting back, we hoped, not too long into the night.

Little did I know what was transpiring in a suite in Vegas.

The best baseball general managers identify the guy or guys they want, and they do everything they can within reason to get them. It's not that complicated, but you would be surprised how many take the passive approach. This was one of the reasons Friedman is so good. He saw what I could do, how I would fit into his team, and he made his move, which included meeting me face-to-face.

And while it would seem to be common sense to meet the player in person—out of uniform—to talk, observe, and digest, you would be surprised how many decision-makers don't take that approach. You have executives who think they can get a read on a player simply by looking at some analytics, and maybe hearing some sort of scuttlebutt from one of their scouts to paint what they probably think is a pristine picture. Not Andrew.

Friedman did his homework, understood what I was all about, and also valued looking me eye to eye before talking numbers. He took the right approach. He didn't want to fall short. He didn't want the second or third choice because he understood that was no way to live life as a team-builder. What happens when you lose because you fell just short with your top priority, having to ride with the second or third option? That is a reality the Dodgers' brass seemed to grasp thoroughly.

So, by the time the rubber was ready to meet the road in Vegas, the Dodgers had shown their interest, and we had recip-rocated. Now came the cat-and-mouse. We couldn't tip our hand that we viewed the Dodgers as the be-all, end-all, but we also couldn't risk missing this opportunity for fear of needing to turn to teams that were further down the list.

The Dodgers also had to realize that'd I'd join them at what they viewed as palatable terms. Sure, they had gone down the laundry list of reasons why I was their guy, but they had other laundry lists and other guys, as well.

So, starting about midnight Vegas time, the games began, with Sam and Seth telling Friedman nobody was leaving until there was a deal done. (And there were a lot of people on both sides hunkering down in that suite.)

Among the Dodgers posse Friedman rolled in with was a former ACES client, Raúl Ibañez, who was now working with the club. Seth and Sam were supposed to feel the presence of Ibañez, along with the five other Dodgers executives. So, the Levinsons countered, hailing another one of their guys, former Red Sox third baseman Mike Lowell, to hang out. They weren't about to be outnumbered.

"I thought we were playing cards," Lowell said upon entering the room. Little did he know that for a good chunk of the next six hours he would be privy to what Seth later told his son Zack (who was also in the suite) was one of the most unusual, all-night negotiating sessions the longtime agents had ever experienced. And, believe me, they had experienced a lot.

They offered two years. We thought they were crazy. We asked for four years. They thought we were nuts. And so it went. From our end, we had stats and stats and stats, and, more important, that last image against the Dodgers.

About three in the morning, my phone rang. It was Seth. "We're close. Not quite there yet, but close. Keep the ringer on." Free agency can be fun . . . until it isn't. This was somewhere in between.

Finally, at about 6:30 a.m., I got the call. The Dodgers had agreed to three years and a club option for $25 million. And, to make it official, the two sides had documented the arrangement on a napkin. Yes, all of those years of ups and downs and hard work was now immortalized on one of the last remaining unsoiled items in that suite.

True to their proclamation more than six hours earlier, Friedman and the Levinsons made sure a deal was done before anybody left that suite. Baseball careers aren't easy, and neither are the moments that help punctuate them. Another Vegas all-nighter proved that.

Three years later, we were back at it. Same open market, dramatically different landscape.

Whereas before I was hitting free agency shot out of the cannon that was a World Series win and career-altering postseason run, this time would be different. My evolution with the Dodgers had been what I was hoping for when coming away from that first meeting with Friedman—winning another World Series while playing a key role in all three of my seasons with Los Angeles.

But there was that matter of a torn biceps during the 2021 postseason that put a damper on my free agent optimism. I wasn't the first or last player to brace himself for the uncomfortable feeling that comes with an uneven last impression heading into the open market. So be it. I was ready to show whatever team that signed me it was going to be a big winner.

As the lockout ended, there were a couple of one-year offers and a couple of two-year offers but from clubs that I did not expect to be serious playoff contenders. I wasn't going to be ready for Opening Day, so I got it. But then came that call while I was cruising through the Miguel's Jr. for some Mexican food.

It was Seth. "The White Sox are the best club, and they are offering you two years and have now distinguished themselves from the competition."

What?!

Through all the teams that I had heard were showing interest, not once was Chicago brought up. The Cubs? Yes. The White Sox? Nope.

The first thing I thought of was how weird it was that just the day before I was telling someone that the White Sox had the sickest uniforms in the major leagues. In fact, they were neck-and-neck with the Raiders for best in all of sports. There was something about that badass black-and-white.

Uniforms weren't going to be the difference-maker, but having a good one never hurts.

It's funny to think back on how your priorities change since those first few years in Little League. Back then, the uniform could be everything. "I'm not going to play for that team because they have lousy uniforms!" That is something a kid would say.

Even jersey numbers. Some guys obsess over making sure they can secure their lucky digits in whatever team they're going to. Not me. When I went to the Red Sox I was going to wear No. 58 because that's what they gave me in St. Louis when I showed up as a rookie. (Back then, they never let you pick your number.) But Jonathan Papelbon, a favorite closer in Boston up until 2011, had worn that number so I went with No. 56. In Little League and high school my numbers were always five or six, with my dad having worn No. 6 as a football player at Vanderbilt.

Now, it's No. 17. Why? Because that's what they gave me in college and it seemed to work out pretty well back then. Digits on the back of a uniform were never going to be part of any negotiations.

All I want is a jersey top where the sleeve isn't too long so it doesn't get caught up on my elbow, and tight pants because that's how I wear my regular clothes. Justin Turner might insist on a presentation that includes two buttons always unbuttoned, a cut undershirt, and pine tar on his right shoulder every single time. But that's not me.

Still, I'm not going to lie. I did like some badass black-and-white uniform.

The second thing I thought of after being hit with flashbacks to my recent uniform conversation was . . . "Holy crap, La Russa!"

I knew the White Sox's Tony La Russa from when he was a special assistant to Dave Dombrowski during our 2018 championship season in Boston. Obviously, everybody understood what he represented in the game of baseball—the Hall of Fame manager who first managed the White Sox at the age of thirty-four back in 1979 and went on to win championships with both Oakland and St. Louis. He was an innovator, and yet he was still old school.

In some ways, Tony was the big league version of my youth baseball coach Rich Krzysiak. "Tough nuts, kick butts!" I knew what La Russa wanted, and he knew I could deliver.

There was no hemming or hawing. No demand for a medical evaluation. The White Sox had a need—a reliever who could pitch on the big stage, had a championship pedigree, was fearless, and could pitch in the back end of their bullpen when the lights were the brightest. I was checking off all their boxes.

The White Sox, a club that I believed could play deep into October, appeared completely out of nowhere.

Two hours. Give us two hours. That's all we asked, just to do due diligence that some of these other interested parties were going to jump up and make a case like the White Sox were. Nope. I looked at Ashley. She looked at me. And just as the order of Mexican food arrived, we came to the conclusion: Chicago was going to be our next stop.

St. Louis. Boston. Los Angeles. Chicago. How lucky am I?

The dollars, cents, and suspensions can get complicated. But, for me, it always comes back to those words from one of my favorite players of all time, Ken Griffey Jr.: "It's a game, and that's how I am going to treat it."

Me, too.

CHAPTER SIX

OFF THE FIELD

O slider slide
O slider slide
Past the batsman I send my slider to hide
O slider slide o slider slide
Past the batsmen I send that round cowhide
O slider slide o slider slide
A fortune staked on you lest I over stride
O slider slide o slider slide
In the strike zone indeed a win is implied
O slider slide o slider slide
The humans can't believe my 3000rpm and fastball ride
O slider slide o slider slide
Your execution can earn you a bride
O slider slide o slider slide
Even the backup tried
O slider slide o slider slide
To the back foot of a lefty . . . check swing and the ump is wrong.

—DYLAN EDWARD CEASE

• • •

This is a poem written by an actual Major League Baseball player. It's a really good poem, and he's a really good player. And before most of Dylan's starts throughout 2022, he would grace us with a dramatic reading of this work of art.

Who knew such creative things could exist in baseball? We did.

Everyone has strengths and weaknesses. That is a fact of life that baseball puts on display every time the ballpark gates open up, televisions are turned on, and video clips surface through your social media platform of choice. That is the act of throwing, catching, and hitting a ball. A closer look into any baseball player's existence will usually reveal something the public had no idea was a thing.

Did people know Dylan Cease was a poet? Probably not a lot.

And this is perhaps our game's biggest challenge, making sure sports fans understand these players are not only human beings, they are humans whom you might be interested in beyond the basics of a baseball field.

Major League Baseball players actually do have personalities. Who knew? Well, the players do. Now we're just waiting for the teams to let the rest of the world see us and realize it as well.

It has been pathetic how reluctant some of these teams—and Major League Baseball—have been when it comes to getting out the very simple message that could have a very real impact on stripping away boredom from baseball. It should make all the sense in the world to scream from the mountaintops that your product has personality. Not to MLB.

Heck, I guarantee a big part of the reason the St. Louis Cardinals traded me to the Red Sox back in 2014 was because I had too much personality. They didn't feel I was focused on baseball.

How can Kelly possibly have fun and play this game at a high level? they thought. I 100 percent guarantee that was a huge part of the equation when deciding to ship me to Boston.

In fairness, the Cardinals weren't—and aren't—alone in that archaic way of thinking. Case in point, when I went over to a radio station at my first Winter Weekend with the Red Sox and predicted I was going to win the American League Cy Young Award, the Sox people weren't thrilled and told me so. Talk about fastball grips or workout regimens, great. But get a little loose with some good-natured bravado, let's reel it in.

And therein lies the problem.

These teams have been telling their players from day one to be scared shitless when it comes to showing off their personality. Flat out, the teams are way too protective. Give basic answers. Don't talk about specific injuries. And, whatever you do, don't engage on social media. Then the players start buying into it, making sure they protect their brand at all costs. Well, all of that is over! At least it needs to be.

Why get all these rookies in a room and convince them that the best way to live as a professional baseball player is by putting up a wall around them and only answering questions about how to throw a split-finger fastball? Instead, start putting money into taking the exact opposite approach. Let's lean into the chaos that comes with all our personalities with social media campaigns, television shows, and internet creativity.

The blueprints aren't hard to find. Forget about the NBA, NFL, and NHL—all of whom are doing a better job than MLB when it comes to pushing their personalities. Focus on a guy named Max Homa.

Homa was a guy who lost his card on the PGA Tour in 2017 after making only two cuts in seventeen events. He made a grand total of $18,008. But, you know what? People cared about him. You know why? Because he actually showed his personality on social media and became a conversation starter, even as his golf game went down the tubes. The combination of self-deprecation ("Had a few caddies hit me up recently, hoping to team up. They heard they usually get weekends off, which is apparently a great selling point," he once tweeted) and entertainment had sports fans pulling for him. Now? He has 350,000 Twitter followers, and he's been adopted by fan bases who care more about the nineteenth hole than one through eighteen—such as the Barstool Sports crew—while bringing lots of folks into what had been the boring world of golf.

Baseball needs to let its players learn from Max.

It's not as if MLB doesn't have a smattering of hope when it comes to taking some steps in the right direction. I lived it with the Dodgers. They are on the trolley. Ever heard of the TV series *Backstage: Dodgers*? You should. Everyone should. This production—which isn't just the cookie-cutter-sponsored promotional video—is a great example of how, with a little more money, a lot more access, and actually prioritizing the showcase of human interaction, the conversation and interest can amp up in a hurry.

Think HBO's *Hard Knocks* series and you have an idea of what *Backstage: Dodgers* is all about. It's highly produced and highly entertaining, and it's also amazing how MLB isn't finding a way for this sort of thing to be in front of every sports fan in every market. Who knew that my going to Jerry's Barber Shop—one of the episodes on the show—would be part of any solution to this baseball-isn't-boring revolution, but it was.

They show up at my house. They ride in my car. They watch me talk with my son. And, finally, they put some actual money into the production of the finished product. The next thing I know, I have people coming up to me saying they had little interest in watching baseball, but now they actually care when I pitch. It's a simple equation. Why can't Major League Baseball see that?

It's slowly starting to change. But baseball needs to kick it into another gear.

It's on us, as well.

It's not easy putting yourself out there. Players understand that. I certainly understand that. In the big leagues, I was probably first introduced to that balancing act that comes with being authentic in front of thousands and thousands of onlookers during Game 6 of the 2013 National League Championship Series.

For two months leading into that elimination game, I had done the same thing when it came to standing out in front of the dugout for the national anthem. I was always going to be the last player to break off from the lineup and come back to the dugout. At first it was just to be a smart-ass, then it became something I and my Cardinal teammates came to expect. I was not heading back to our guys until the opposing team had completely returned to its respective bench.

So, when this game came around—the one that if we won would punch our ticket to the World Series—I didn't think anything about what kind of stage we were standing on. I had no concept of how many television viewers were tuning in or the importance of the baseball that would be on display. All I knew was that I had to do what I had been doing—being the last to leave the national anthem lineup.

My rallying cry was, "We already won the game today, boys, because they lost the anthem!"

But this time there was a problem. The Dodgers' Scott Van Slyke was taking it upon himself to outlast me. So, there were the two of us, hats over hearts, all by ourselves in front of our respective teams. Suddenly, I realized what I had gotten myself into. Van Slyke wasn't moving, and, to make matters worse, he was much closer to his dugout whereas I was a good fifteen feet out on the dirt, adding to my increasing feeling of isolation.

What was fun and games for all those previous pregame rituals now was starting to weigh heavy on me. This was Game 6 of the National League Championship Series, and I was basically serving as a statue for millions to gawk at.

Then, just when I started questioning me imitating the Queen's Guard at Buckingham Palace, I heard my manager, Mike Matheny. He was usually pretty stoic and businesslike, sticking to the by-the-book approach with such things as pregame routines.

After a quick smile, Mike said, "You stay out there until you win!"

I knew right then and there, leaving before Van Slyke—who was also getting threats from his teammates to not break off from his stance—was not an option.

So, we stood, and we stood, and we stood. Our starting pitcher, Michael Wacha, and the rest of our starters took the field and started warming up for the biggest game of most of our lives, all with me and Van Slyke still maintaining our position—hats still covering our hearts, staring straight ahead.

Finally, home plate umpire Greg Gibson took his mask off, stepped in front of home plate, and yelled to both of us, "Everybody at the same time, let's go," motioning his arms as he waved us off the field. So, I took a couple of steps to the dugout just to deck Van Slyke, and then came back. But Scott took my movements as an opportunity to claim victory, and eased into a collection of cheering Dodgers. If that made them feel good to suggest they had won, so be it. They didn't win. I won. We won—twice, first with the national anthem and then on the scoreboard a few hours later.

"What a weird way to start Game 6," Joe Buck uttered on national TV after I finally left the field, raising my hat to the cheering Cardinals fans.

Yes, it was awkward and even somewhat embarrassing. But it was unforgettable. Baseball needs more of that, those personality-driven events that players are sometimes reluctant to engage in.

If opportunities present themselves, you have to jump on them. Baseball is, after all, about opportunities.

In 2013 when we found an old-man mask lying around, we put it to good use by fooling the musician Nelly that he was being grilled by a kindly, really, really old fan named Phineas.

"I heard you're an athlete, but I would like to race you some day. I'm ninety-two and I could still beat you in a race." He seemed befuddled. And Nelly's confusion only got worse when I started rapping through my newly wrinkled face "H to the Izzo," which was not one of his songs. Even when I revealed myself, the St. Louis native seemed a bit confused, probably, I thought, because he had no idea who Joe Kelly was.

But then, eight years later, at Mookie Betts's wedding, I heard someone yell, "Kell!" It was Nelly. "Man, you got me with that mask." It took a while, but thanks to my movie prop chicanery and Mookie's nuptials, Nelly and I became fast friends. The power of baseball hijinks!

Five years after the Nelly prank, I went back into wardrobe, this time to play the part of an older reporter from the local TV station in Punta Gorda, Florida. I roamed through the Red Sox spring training, with none of my teammates knowing it was me who was calling David Ortiz "Big Poopy" or walking out onto the field in the middle of drills without a care in the world.

Heaven forbid, we actually have a good time while living the life of a baseball player.

It's all there to be had. Now it's about who is going to follow suit and start letting their guard down.

Players have all these emotions and thoughts going through their heads, but none of these thoughts, emotions, or words ever come to the light of the media, the light of day. They might say it on a podcast, but usually it isn't even the one they're attached to. They're usually hiding from questions and avoiding what they really want to say. What they have to realize is the world has changed. There is an acceptance of people, including athletes, being more vocal. It's not frowned upon anymore, and it shouldn't be.

But, for some reason, most players are still frightened.

So, what are they afraid of? I think a lot of them are petrified of repercussions from their team or the fear of people not liking them. But that thought process should be outdated. People like when you're genuine, when you're speaking like you're in a regular conversation. That's how I approach it, and the whole game of baseball would be viewed in a better light if other guys followed suit.

Take for instance when I went to a Chicago radio station after Josh Donaldson called my teammate Tim Anderson "Jackie" after Jackie Robinson. I called Donaldson a douche for saying what most people perceived as a wildly inappropriate comment. So, why did I call him a douche? Because only a person who is a douche would say something like that. Only people who are bad human beings say something like that.

Most people wouldn't have something like that go through their head. So, for me, it was simple. I called Donaldson a douche because he was one.

"Oooh."

"Aaaah."

"I can't believe Joe said that."

"Joe, you shouldn't say that."

There was some of that, but for me it's not that complicated—why make it so? Yes, most players would dance around it, but they're thinking the same thing. Why not just speak the truth? It's life. That's what it is. Who cares, right? I'm going to say it because that's who I have been my whole life. If I know something is right to say, I'm going to say it. I don't give a fuck, and neither should all these other players saying the same thing.

Think about it. So, you get pushback. That's the worst people have to deal with, protecting their brand. What does that even mean? You have to deal with social media? Only in America are people saying that. There are wars going on forcing ten people to live in a twenty-square-foot room. Here you're worried about someone making fun of you or someone wanting to fight you. Fight them. What's the worst that can happen? You get punched in the face? It's going to hurt. Oh, well.

Why are people so worried about all these outside factors when you know what you're doing and saying is right? I work hard. I'm a good teammate. I'm a good parent. I'm a good husband. I'm a good son. Why should I be worried about my brand? If that's what you're worried about, instead of actually playing the game or going out and living your life, then you have more problems than just me.

Ruin your brand. Keep ruining it. If people think you're a bad guy, then be the bad guy in their eyes all the time. As long as you know what's right. The greatest players in the world are hated by fans. Tom Brady is the best to ever do it and people still hate him.

You can't be liked by everyone, so why do you keep trying? It only matters if you care about it. Pick the five things that you care about the most, and after that nothing else matters.

When it comes to rebranding baseball, that's a good place to start. Think about all the other sports, how honesty and openness have leaked into their way of doing things. It seems like baseball is last.

When I do something on the field, like when I raised my arms to the Yankees' Aaron Hicks after picking him off second base in a May game at Yankee Stadium, it wasn't to show anybody up or create some sort of meme. It was just my authentic reaction, as if to say to him, "What are you doing?" It's the reaction I would have given my son, my brothers, my teammates, or even my wife. "What the hell, Ashley? Why would you do that?" It's just me being me. You can hate it. Oh, well. I'm not going to lose any sleep, and neither should others who are simply trying to be themselves.

Just look at the interviews guys are doing. Not enough guys have felt free enough to speak their minds. You're not going to change the guys who are introverts, and that's fine. This is all about being yourself. But if you do have it in you, let it out. You see guys who act totally different when the mics are off than they do when they're on. Why? Baseball players are humans. We have good days and bad days, so when things go south and somebody asks how you felt today, instead of saying you missed your spots and you have to go back and look at the tape, or your mechanics were off, what's wrong with responding like a normal person would? "My arm hurts like hell. I took 1,000 milligrams of ibu-profen before this game. I have been hanging a bit, and I was bound to give up at least one of these." So, there you go.

How you act off the field and outside the clubhouse should be how you act on the field and inside the clubhouse. If we could get to a place in this game where every player is comfortable existing and not acting, baseball will automatically take a step forward.

Let's just have some fun. Please!

Play baseball. Have some fun. Be around the guys. Have some fun. Interviews with the media. Have some fun. Go to the White House. Yup. Have some fun.

The honor of visiting with the president and vice president of the United States is an honor little skateboarding Joe Kelly could have never imagined would be possible. But there it was, a second invitation to 1600 Pennsylvania Avenue, and this time I was actually able to attend. Let's go!!!

The first go-round—when the Red Sox celebrated their 2018 world championship during an early-season swing through Baltimore—I couldn't make the trip since, by the time of the invitation, I was playing for a completely different team. I had witnessed the annual rite of passage for championship teams in past years, remembering Jonny Gomes's red, white, and blue sport coat and David Ortiz's impromptu selfie with Barack Obama. So, I had a pretty good idea what to expect. That didn't mean this had to be a gray suit, nice-to-meet-you, get-on-the-bus exercise.

Baseball is all about making memories, so that's exactly what I did when visiting the White House a few months after our 2020 world championship with the Dodgers.

The first order of business was finding some pants. Heading to Washington, DC, from Los Angeles, I was somewhat ill-prepared considering I hadn't packed any suitable pants. So, I turned to my teammate Mookie Betts.

I remembered Mookie had the same waste size as me and had worn these dope blue suit pants on Opening Day. I asked him if he had them kicking around. His wife, Brianna, was nice enough to jet them over to the clubhouse before we left, with the slacks waiting for me in my locker after our game and before he took off for Washington, DC.

That day, my fashion universe aligned.

Mookie's pants, while a tad bit shorter than I was used to, were fire. I woke up with my mullet popping just right. And the mustache was serving as a perfect complement to the entire package. And then there was the jacket. Remember that trade I made with that mariachi musician for that jacket? Well, this was going to be the ultimate payoff.

Mariachi Joe was headed to the White House.

I have a couple credos I tell everyone in baseball to abide by: Don't look back, and don't be afraid to be different. But I would be lying if I said I wasn't a bit sheepish when it came to what kind of reaction I was going to get from my teammates upon entering the breakfast banquet room at the hotel before our trip to the House of the People. Elevator doors open. I walk in. It was better than I imagined. All my Dodgers teammates and the executives from the club were applauding, laughing, and asking for photos. We were there to celebrate, and my jacket had become the party starter.

But friends and family were one thing, the Secret Service was another.

As I got off the bus and walked into the White House, I could hear the murmuring with each person I passed by, feeling like all eyes were on me and not always in a good way.

Once inside, we went to a room where we were scheduled to shake hands with Vice President Kamala Harris. Standing next to Walker Buehler, I turned to him and said, "I'm going to introduce myself as 'Joe "Two-Time" Kelly,' because I've been invited to the White House two times, one more than she had. Here she comes." I couldn't back down.

"Nice to meet you, Madam Vice President. I'm Joe 'Two-Time' Kelly. 'Two-Time' because I have been invited to the White House one more time than you have."

The vice president hesitated a few seconds, soaking in the introduction. And then, without hardly altering her expression or skipping a beat, she responded, "Nice to meet you, 'Two-Time.'" There was clearly pride in the vice president's face, and laughter everywhere from anyone within earshot of the introduction.

Now it was time to meet President Joe Biden, who was only shaking hands with about six players—all of whom had already been COVID cleared to even touch the president. I once again told Buehler that, if I was given the chance, the president was also going to be introduced to "Two-Time." So, standing about five people down from President Biden and one row back, while posing for the team photo, I leaned in. "Nice to meet you, President Biden. My name is Joe 'Two-Time' Kelly. 'Two-Time' because I have been invited to the White House twice, just like you."

While the introduction once again left my teammates buckled over, it didn't quite take with the president. What it did do was put me on the radar of those protecting him.

After President Biden's speech, one of our trainers came up to me and said, "Bro, you're not going to believe what just happened. That Secret Service guy was just asking about you." He went on to explain how my guy was called over by this protector of the president, took out his earpiece, and said: "This is off the record. What's up with your boy over in the jacket? Is he OK? Why is he walking around in that jacket?"

The trainer's response was one of befuddlement. "Joe? Yeah, of course."

I legit had the Secret Service sweating. I knew I was being watched. It turns out that the folks in the White House weren't all that different from a good chunk of baseball. They could surely go for a more regular dose of this kind of fun.

Another reminder the White House trip supplied was about fashion. It's a very real part of sports fandom that baseball is just starting to catch on to.

Uniforms. Cleats. Gloves. Accessories. For years, MLB wanted to dumb it all down. And I'll admit it now—I was brainwashed. Well, I'm not denying it anymore. Back in my initial run-through in professional baseball, I was not helping the cause when it came to growing the game.

Team over personality. That was what I was taught, and I totally bought in.

If a player on the other team came out on the field dripping with jewelry or wearing his uniform in some sort of unique fashion, I immediately jumped to the conclusion that he had no discipline. He didn't respect the moment. He wasn't going to succeed because that's simply not how a baseball player presented himself.

That's the way it was. At least that is how the Cardinals taught me.

Coming up through the minor leagues, the message was clear. Everyone had to look relatively the same. Interviews? Here are the talking points. Make sure you wear your pants up in the same manner for each and every game.

And once you did get to the big leagues, forget about spending more than just a few minutes wearing too much jewelry in the inner sanctum that is the clubhouse. Once you get into that uniform, don't even think about distinguishing yourself from everyone else. And if you do, you better brace yourself for a ration of shit from 90 percent of the team.

This was something that was policed. And, you know what? I ultimately became one of the guys keeping an eye out for those going rogue.

But you know what else? Dude, it's a game. A game! What were we doing?

Polos on the road. Dress shoes all the time. Everything was so uptight. It wasn't until about 2018 when we started seeing things turn, which I witnessed firsthand thanks to Alex Cora allowing us to wear sweat suits on the plane rides. Gasp! Thinking back to how bizarrely strict all that stuff was is mind-boggling.

What teams and Major League Baseball were trying to do was treat their players like they were in the Army. That works in the Army, because discipline and consistency are essential to the work it does. There's no messing around, and everybody better be on the same page. Understood.

But we're playing a game. It's not the same.

Baseball stumbled upon its path to sanity with that first Players' Weekend in 2017, when all of a sudden guys could wear nicknames on the back of their uniforms and any color cleats they wanted. It was just a few days, but it opened a lot of eyes as to how silly the other 159 games were.

Now, the reins have been loosened and baseball is coming around to where the other leagues have already been thriving. We have a long way to go, but at least we're starting to see the errors of our ways.

It's a novel concept: Be yourself and have fun. You can do it, baseball.

CHAPTER SEVEN

THE COMMISSIONER SPEAKS

When I walked into that conference room with some of my White Sox teammates back in early March 2022, I was fired up. I was ready to throw down, at least verbally.

A group of us had been selected to meet with Major League Baseball Commissioner Rob Manfred, who was not one of my favorite people. And in the world of big-league ballplayers, I wasn't alone.

Not only had we just gone through all the vitriol that came with a lockout by the owners—with Manfred serving as their spokesman—but I had my own history. Two times I had been suspended in what I viewed as less-than-ideal fashion, and while the commish wasn't in the room for either pre-suspension confrontation, he represented what I perceived as a big part of the problem.

There were other sticking points when it came to the perception of Manfred, with the last straw for many of the guys coming when he matter-of-factly called the World Series championship trophy a piece of metal back before the 2020 season. The fact that the commissioner was actually devaluing the Commissioner's Trophy—which was the one thing we as players work our whole career to hold at the end of a baseball season—was incomprehensible. And sticking the dagger in a little further was that he uttered such a thing in defense of his decision not to strip the Astros of their title—the championship they stole from the Dodgers— which only infuriated my then-Dodgers teammates more.

Let's just say that Justin Turner is not a fan. And neither am I.

So, now Manfred was trying to extend an olive branch to all the teams after what had become another two steps back for baseball—the lockout. He was traveling to meet with all thirty teams, with a select group of players from each club allowed to have it out with the commissioner. My blood was pumping. I was ready to air some serious grievances.

I came into that room saying, "Screw this guy."

An hour later, I was walking out in a completely different frame of mind than I had entered with. It was not what I expected.

The first smart step by Manfred was bringing Raúl Ibañez along as his plus-one. Raúl was a respected former player, whom I not only knew from working with the Dodgers but also because we shared the same agents—Sam and Seth Levinson. He knew how hot I was running and that it was important to defuse the animosity from the get-go.

Then Manfred started talking.

This sixty-three-year-old, whom I had viewed as just another suit, more concerned with bottom lines than the actual game of baseball, immediately put me on my heels. He was apologetic. He was sympathetic. And he was informative.

What started as Manfred's mea culpa—explaining that the "piece of metal" comment and the subsequent us-against-them environment were problems he owned and wanted to learn from—turned to questions posed to us about how to actually fix this game.

It became a conversation, the likes of which our game desperately needs.

"Hey, man. The game has to change. Why are these other sports so far ahead of us?" I asked. There were other questions and concerns. Why couldn't we find owners—like Mark Cuban or Steve Ballmer—who actually seem like fans, instead of a bunch of old, rich people? What's up with the rules changes? Stuff like that.

Maybe it was in my own head, but it sure seemed like even though there were about a dozen people in this room, Manfred and I were locked on each other. Perhaps it was because we acknowledged the animosity between us and that patching up our wounds was going to go a long way toward the greater good. Whatever his approach, the meeting worked.

When the hour was done, we all had a better understanding of one another. Manfred certainly knew what was gnawing at us players, and he had presented himself in a much clearer light.

Could he just flat-out decree that rules were changing and the players would simply have to adjust? Of course. But Manfred had convinced us that he did want to pass these ideas through us and the changing of the game was going to be more along the lines of the collaboration we were hoping for.

The bottom line was that both sides sitting in that room understood the game we loved had issues and needed some saving.

A few months later, I checked in with Manfred again. The sting of the lockout had dissipated, and the realization of all that was right with the world had trickled back, thanks to the 2022 season. I wanted to keep the conversations going with the commissioner, continuing to better understand where he was coming from.

So, we met up again . . .

ME: Good to talk to you again. One of the things I was wondering after getting together back in Arizona was how you actually first fell in love with the game of baseball.

MANFRED: Well, you know, my first game was August 10, 1968. I was ten years old, and it was a big deal, living in upstate New York, a place called Rome, and going to a Yankees game. My older sister, my younger brother, and my whole family came down for it. My dad was a big Yankees fan and I was a huge Mickey Mantle fan, and it was his last season. So, we go down to the Stadium and it's Old-Timers' Day. I remember vividly walking into that ballpark. It was incredible. First you had the Old-Timers' game and then the regular game—they were playing the Twins—and Mickey hit a home run from each side. We stayed over at some Howard Johnson's in Westchester and were going to a game the next day as well. So, I'm thinking this is how it works, go to the game and the Yankees win, especially with Mel Stottlemyre pitching. His ERA was sitting in the twos, and he was having his best year. Well, nope. He gave up seven runs in

1 2/3 innings. But, I mean, it was still such a great weekend and really cemented my love for the game, which I had just started playing in Little League. It was just such a great family trip and left a huge impression on me. That kind of started my love for baseball.

ME: That's awesome. I actually had a somewhat similar thing happen to me. My favorite player growing up was Ken Griffey Jr., and I was able to go to a Dodgers game when he played for the Reds. We were sitting down in left field, and he hit a foul ball right in front of where me, my dad, and my brothers were all sitting, like two seats in front. It bounces right up to me and lands like a foot away, and I'm so excited. As I'm reaching down, a guy my dad's age was reaching down and I end up grabbing his hand instead of the ball and he gets it. I didn't know what to do. I started getting teary-eyed and just felt completely lost. I was so irritated that my dad didn't wrestle that ball away from that guy, especially because it was hit by my favorite player. I never forgot that moment just because that was my absolute favorite player. I thought I was never going to have a chance for something like that again. But then after we won the World Series with the Dodgers, Griffey made a video for me, because he found out he was my favorite player. That was epic.

MANFRED: Ken is just such an awesome guy. We showed a video at the owners' meetings where there is a young kid who has an incident playing high school baseball. Instead of just calling the kid, Ken flies to South Carolina, spends the afternoon with the young man, and delivers an invitation to the Hank Aaron Invitational in Vero Beach. I mean, it was awesome. There is no other word for it. He is just such a great person, a great human being.

ME: Okay, something that struck me. You are one of four people in this country running a major sports league, which is wild to think about. I was wondering how you view these other leagues—the NBA, NFL, and NHL— and how they are run and what we can take away from the successes and failures of the other sports and the people who run them.

MANFRED: So, I think the biggest challenge for us, Joe, is that our reach right now is not great because of the erosion of the cable TV bundle. I'm going to give you one number: If you take the home television territories and all those homes that are available, we are able to broadcast into 32 percent of those homes. So, how do you fix it? We have to deliver digital alternatives to people outside the bundle, allowing fans a greater ability to watch what they want to watch as they need. I mean, this is the single biggest issue. This is a really, really important piece of the puzzle.

When you're watching something—whether it's on TV or some digital offering or whatever—it is like an entrée into the game. So, little kids see it because their parents present it to them and then they want to play it. Then they will want to go to the ballpark. None of it will happen if they don't see it at home, and because it is so limited, we are missing that generation. We're completely missing it.

ME: I know exactly what you're talking about. My wife and kids went back from Chicago to our home in LA, where we had canceled our cable, and they couldn't find the games anywhere. My six-year-old was pissed. He was like, "I'm going to the game, because I can't watch it anywhere." My wife, meanwhile, is trying to juggle three kids, so she can't watch him all the time. That's just a small example, but I totally get what you're talking about. It's not good. The cable thing is a problem.

MANFRED: It's a huge problem.

ME: This is an example of the interest in baseball being down, but it's down not because it wants to be down. It's down because it's handcuffed, so, it looks like it's down.

MANFRED: That's exactly right. The business model is broken.

ME: They are taking numbers on face value. They're not looking into it. They're just saying baseball is boring and nobody is watching. Well, no. People in the home markets of the NFL and NBA, they're not getting blacked out.

MANFRED: Their business is better, and we have to fix ours. The upside? I would say this—and the commissioners of the other sports wouldn't say this out loud but probably realize it—our live product is the best in sports, I believe. I really do. That's the upside for us. But I would say this: I do think we have to stabilize the way we're playing the game. We need consistency in the way we're playing the game. We should make sure we're putting forth the best form of baseball. Action. Moving things along. All those good things.

ME: I think the players are on board with all of that. That said, I'm curious if there was anyone you talked to, or even a moment you talked to someone who truly gave you that "Aha!" moment, where it became so clear that something had to be done or how something should be done?

MANFRED: I'll tell you two things. First, at one of the owners' meetings, we put Game 7 of the 1960 World Series—the Bill Mazeroski walk-off homer game—up side by side with Game 7 of the 2016 World Series. There was the exact same number of runs scored in both games, so we put them next to each other to compare. That was the only thing similar between the two. The one from 1960 was about two hours shorter. There were fourteen strikeouts in the 2016 game, while not a single batter struck out in the Mazeroski game. The one back fifty-six years before had a ton more balls put in play, with batters swinging at the first pitch all over the place. There was clearly a dramatic difference. It all really made us think, *What has happened here?*

What happened here is that you got a lot of smart people with a lot of analytics, and they all started focusing on one thing: They want to win one more game. We let the process dictate how the games are being played. That's ass-backward. We should play the game the way that is good for the fans.

ME: Yup. We aren't playing a game called *baseball* anymore. We're playing a game called *run prevention*. We're not playing to win, we're playing to limit runs. I think that screwed up what should have been an entertaining evolution of the game.

MANFRED: I agree. Perfect. And one more thing: This run prevention, pitch away from contact, maximum effort has ruined a lot of careers.

ME: And remember when starting pitchers used to be the be-all and end-all? They were the guys everyone came to see. Not anymore. Chris Carpenter. Jake Westbrook. Those are the guys I strived to be. Seven, eight innings. That was what we wanted. Let them go. I love that. Not anymore. I look into this stuff. Everyone is changing because they feel like they have to. Guys I played with who were throwing four-seam fastballs at the top of the strike zone every single time are not throwing changeups and two-seamers. With no sticky stuff, all these guys are trying to learn changeups because, you know why? You can't throw a changeup with sticky stuff. All of it is different and not all of it is good. I miss the idea of those stud starting pitchers. It's a joke.

MANFRED: I know you are so right because I have guys, who will remain nameless, who would give me half their salary if they could be out there using pine tar every day.

ME: Oh, yeah. One hundred percent. Everybody wants to do it. The lack of pine tar just exploits the flaws in pitching mechanics.

MANFRED: There is a marketing element to this, as well. The biggest stars in our game used to be starting pitchers. You're not getting three times through the order? I mean, it's terrible.

ME: It's so bad for the game. I used to look at starting pitchers like icons. I mean, they were larger than life. When I met Chris Carpenter, I was like, "Holy shit!" There are no Chris Carpenters on the Tampa Bay Rays. There are no starting pitchers on a lot of teams in baseball now.

MANFRED: It doesn't happen.

ME: So what do we do? How do we start chipping away at this? How do we get baseball to actually succeed, No. 1, on the field, and No. 2, with this new age of instant-gratification sports fans? They want action as soon as a guy steps in the box. How can we position ourselves for the new age of sports fans?

MANFRED: All right, I think you know some of this is blocking and tackling. We're spending a lot of money on that because simply getting kids to play is really important. You have to get kids to play. No. 2, our broadcast product needs to look different. On the digital side, it needs to be more national. If you're a White Sox fan in LA, you need to be able to watch on a platform that is flexible enough so anybody can watch what they want to watch. What do I mean by that? If you want to get every save opportunity for every game, you can buy that and watch them as they unfold across the league. You want to see your favorite player's every at-bat, you can give them that. We have to give the fans a chance to watch what they want to watch.

Here is the buzzword for everything we're doing with our digital products right now: It's *personalization*. Through the ballpark app, we can tell what the fans are doing, who is sitting in what seats, and how often they bought what. We want to know what they're watching and deliver that to the top of their screen, catching their attention to keep them on the site. This is what the Apple deal is all about. It's about partnering with people that can teach you how to deliver things on the digital side. They know. So, look, I'll go back to it, I think a strength for us is that our ballpark experience is better today than it was a decade ago. It's a strength, and it's a strength we have to build on. There is a social aspect to our ballpark experience. That's really good for young people if it's done correctly.

ME: Yeah, 100 percent. Just wrapping things up, going back to our meeting at spring training, guys on our team after that were like, "Holy shit, Rob Manfred is actually cool." I thought you were just coming to talk to us and being authentic was so important. It was a reminder that just because you're commissioner, you literally have your hands in everything, which is dumb. It's just like a president. No matter who it is, that person isn't going to be dealing with every little thing. My question is if the reaction was the same from the other teams? What was the vibe? How did you feel it went? Was every group pretty similar, and what opened your eyes about it all?

MANFRED: I will say this: It was the best idea I have had in a while. It was great. It was uniformly a positive experience. I think probably the biggest takeaway was something I alluded to before. I think for the players, when you talk to them about the way the game is played, they all want one thing. Fundamentally, they simply want consistency. They want the baseball to perform the same every year because they adjust their games to what is going on when they take the field. A lot of it had to do with pitching and the baseball, and what we tried to explain is that everything that has gone on with the baseball has been an effort to make it more consistent. People buy into that, and that has been really important. But I think the dialogue during those meetings and since has been really, really positive. I kicked myself for not getting together sooner.

ME: Listen, we all learn from our mistakes. At least the great ones do. I am constantly looking at other pitchers, trying to figure out things that they are doing that can help me. Do they have an elite pitch or great mechanics that I could tap into, figuring out what their thought process with it might be? I'm just wondering if you— being one of the four big commissioners, you guys are the Big Four—picked up anything from any of those guys? I'm sure you guys have had conversations and plucked ideas from one another.

MANFRED: Sure. Here's an example: Right after I got elected, I really didn't know what to think about this whole gambling thing. I was talking to Adam Silver of the

NBA, and he was telling me, "Look, there are two things: No. 1, go to your lawyers. The law is going to change. You can't stop it. And No. 2, you can defend the integrity of the game as long as you're not at risk, and the fact of the matter is that gambling can be a source of engagement, particularly in a game that has natural breaks like yours." That was influential.

While Manfred directs traffic when it comes to finding the sweet spot for the next wave of baseball fans off the field, there are plenty of players who have taken up the cause while living as big-league ballplayers. Maybe more players than ever.

Social media. Bat flips. Emotion. Spreading the word that baseball is anything but boring.

And when it comes to leading the charge, perhaps there has been no better participant than Brett Phillips.

Brett isn't a superstar, and he has come up playing in the opposite of a big market, Tampa Bay. But he is one of the heroes we need, taking to the streets with his "Baseball Is Fun" marketing campaign, and exhibiting the kind of on-the-field enjoyment fans hope every major leaguer is still fueled by.

So, it only made sense that after talking to the commissioner of baseball, we got the perspective from the commissioner of fun.

Brett Phillips, Baseball Player

So, growing up, I always played multiple sports. I played hockey. I played soccer. And I played baseball. I can recall around the age of nine I was playing travel soccer, and travel baseball started colliding with the tournaments, so I had to make a decision which route I wanted to go. For me it was simple because more of my friends were playing baseball, even though I was pretty good at both at the time. I also really, really enjoyed baseball.

I still remember wearing my baseball uniform underneath my church clothes and my mom looking down and seeing my pants come out from underneath my slacks and being like, "What is that?!" Then being in the car and taking my church clothes off and going to sleep in my uniform. I just loved it so much.

Everyone looks at me and asks why I always look like I'm having so much fun and enjoying myself. Well, I can honestly say that was because of my mom and my dad and my stepdad. My parents never put any additional pressure on me as a kid. After a game, good or bad, we never talked about it. It was never like, "Why did you strike out?" or "How do you think you could have improved?" We never had those conversations. Instead, we were like, "What are we going to eat?" I always tell everyone that I never developed the habit of putting so much pressure on myself, because my parents never put pressure on me. I wouldn't be here without that same mentality. Through all my struggles, I'm always hopeful and always enjoying myself.

All those friends who drifted off from baseball, it usually stemmed from their parents putting way too much additional pressure on them to perform to get better when they're not even on the field. Like being coaches at the house when they're not even the coaches. Sure, when I left the baseball field I still liked hitting and stuff in the backyard. But that was because I just enjoyed it. I didn't have someone telling me to do it. And a lot of that enjoyment stemmed from how encouraging my parents were.

Another big part of baseball, as a kid with ADHD, is that it's always something new. Every single day, it's never the same. The ball is never going to land in the same place. The plays are always going to look different. It's just constantly evolving, and I love that about it.

It allows me to chase that new success every single day, and that's a huge reason why I love baseball so much. It's stimulating. I know for the average fan from the stands there is only action here or there. But I'm telling you, there will always be something you have never seen before. And then there is the camaraderie, growing up with my friends always being there, always experiencing the same fun. That always made baseball so enjoyable.

But, yeah, I would say just the camaraderie, growing up with my friends always there. So that made baseball super enjoyable. I was good at it, and there was also something new every single day. That's why I love it.

There is also the challenge, which I also love. There is the challenge of dealing with the ultimate failure, or just things like the mechanics of pitching and hitting. You can show up after getting it right for three straight days and the next day your mechanics could be completely gone. Dealing with every little detail just when you thought you had figured it out. There is no other sport like that.

You have a 98 mph fastball coming at you, knowing everything has to be perfect with your mechanics just to make contact. And then there is the day-in, day-out mental grind of trying to figure it out. That is baseball.

And now, on top of it all, guys are finally starting to show their personalities more, and actually doing it while in the act of playing baseball. For the longest time everyone was walking on eggshells. This game is hard enough for the young guys, why would we want to make it harder? Yet you had all these older guys throwing around all of these unwritten rules. It was crazy, but it was the reality of it. It's getting better. Obviously, there has to be a level of professionalism and guys have to know right from wrong. But when it comes to guys opening up and showing more personality, that's what fans want to see.

If you look at the NFL or the NBA, those guys have much bigger followings on social media. They want to put themselves out there, see the characters and the personalities. We're getting there, slowly but surely. But we still have to get past some of these unwritten rules of the game. I do think we're getting super close to getting a grasp on it, especially with all these young guys coming up and getting an opportunity. In the past, there was a hierarchy. Sit at your locker and don't talk. But we have to realize that the twenty-one-year-old kid who just got called up is as important as the ten-year veteran. We're all here to win.

But when it comes to getting the personalities out there, it can't be forced. It has to be organic. You see me doing things out there, but it's never premeditated. Like when I pitched in 2021. That was cool and people got a taste of my personality. But, to be honest, the coolest thing for me was the walk-off homer in the World Series. Before that, I was always the funny guy who laughed a lot. The goofball. But then something like that happens, and it kind of bridged the gap between me as the fun-loving, funny guy and me as the "Oh, he can play baseball" guy. People suddenly realized that I'm not just the funny guy, I can also play baseball. I do put in a lot of work, and when you put in a lot of work it can get you those moments. It gave me a lot of confidence.

When it's all said and done, when I'm retired and not playing baseball anymore, I can tell you that I will be able to look myself in the mirror and say: "You enjoyed yourself. You gave it all you had, and you had fun. And you're not going to have any regrets about what is going to happen next." There are a lot of guys who can't do the same, who are retired and salty because they let the game of baseball define them as a person. You strip away baseball from there and who are they? That's the problem. That's not going to be me.

I have had great mentorship, with a lot of good people, friends, and family who have encouraged me. And because of all of it I will never let this game define me because I'm going to have a long life after this. Yeah, I don't want to be that guy who had all of this would-haves, should-haves, could-haves.

I refused to be the guy who wished things were different because I was plagued by anxiety every time I walked on to a field, afraid the veterans were going to say something.

Hey, man. Enjoy. You're a major league player and that could be gone tomorrow. You didn't just sit quietly at your locker. That's not who you were. You went out on the field not caring what people thought and made sure you didn't waste your time. You remembered this was supposed to be fun. That's how I always lived my life and, once again, it's a testament to how I was raised. Don't get me wrong. I'm competitive and want to win as much as anyone. But at the same time, I'm going to enjoy myself.

Everyone should realize how awesome all of this is.

You know, man, I could grow this game by 50 percent easily in one year. Easy. This is what I would say to every major league player across the league: When you were a kid and you went to a baseball game, what's the one thing that made the game fun for you? Well, that would have been meeting a player and getting an autograph. That, for a kid, is the coolest moment ever. It is so cool!

So, what I do every single day is take fifteen to twenty minutes and sign autographs. Every single day. Because I knew as a kid, that's what made the game fun. That kid is going to show up again and again to those games, and it's going to make him fall in love with it, right? Guys just need to understand how quickly they have forgotten that. If you ask a guy how many autographs he signed in a year, it should be more than 162 because that's just one autograph a game. You know what I mean? It seems so simple. But I guarantee for most guys it's less than that.

Let's start waking up and seeing things like that, start giving back. Remembering. I know I will never forget.

CHAPTER EIGHT

WHERE IT ALL BEGINS

One of the great things about baseball is that it peels back pieces of ourselves in the most deliciously unsuspecting ways imaginable. Just a few years ago, a decade after I had first met my wife, Ashley, a few of these revelations started popping up.

First came the origami.

Out of nowhere, I was showing Ashley and our son Knox how to make swans and frogs and such things using paper. The woman who thought she had figured me out was now being introduced to a whole new side of her husband. I knew how to practice the Japanese paper-folding art, which has been around since the early 1600s. For me, it had been in existence since the early 2000s, subtly serving as a perfect complement to my status as stud junior-high baseball player.

When I wanted to break up with girls, they got a nice note folded in origami with a message reading something along the lines of, "I need to focus on playing baseball."

Athlete. Artist. My wife had no idea she'd married such a renaissance man.

Ashley also had absolutely no clue that baseball spawned something besides a way to sever ties with those first few girlfriends. The game also introduced my dancing excellence.

Right around the same time the shock and awe of all that exquisite paper folding was being revealed, we popped in a VHS tape of my first days as a baseball player. She had no idea I had such a propensity for dancing as a six-year-old. And I had no clue I initially viewed baseball through the prism of the film *Footloose*.

The cameras zeroed in on me standing out in the field, dancing away while the coaches furiously tried to organize my tee-ball brethren. There I was, being introduced to the game that would change my life, dancing with the Anaheim Tee-Ball Yankees, a path initiated by my baseball-loving grandfather.

Before wearing that uniform, I had no concept of baseball. My dad was a football guy, and I don't remember ever holding a glove or bat until it was forced on me in between dance moves.

I watch that video, and I wonder what I was thinking, and why I wasn't thinking. There were, after all, the intricacies of the game to learn. Why was I wasting my time jumping up and down aimlessly? Now, I get it.

I now coach these kids. Sure enough, they're dancing and digging in the dirt just like I was.

This has always been the challenge when introducing baseball to any kid, trying to make them realize how much thinking and attention have to go into the spaces between the actual movement. I ultimately got it (although the dancing, in a slightly more subtle form, never totally goes away). But even without the tidal wave of distractions that are presented to this current crop of six-year-olds, the attention span challenge has been a tough nut to crack.

Now that nut has become a rock.

The easy narrative for parents and coaches when it comes to uncovering this attention-span sweet spot is that it is a battle that simply can't be won. We are overmatched by screens, phones, video games, social media, and faster-moving sports with flashier spokespeople. Studies show that the attention span for a five- or six-year-old is twelve to eighteen minutes. There's one inning. And that's not even incorporating those who are just being diagnosed for attention-deficit/hyperactivity disorder.

Oh, well. Baseball had a nice run.

Not so fast.

What I realized when trying to mentor these kids—including my own six-year-old—was that they all were doing the same thing I was, with one difference. While I was frolicking to random music in my own head, these kids were choreographed. These moves were mimicking characters in *Fortnite* or YouTubers or some viral moment that they were passing on to one another. This wasn't random. They were carrying over the source of their distractions to the baseball field. My generation had MTV . . . maybe. Their treasure trove of alternative sources of fun these days is bottomless.

What we have to realize is that it's not all going away.

Can it be frustrating? Sure. I'm sure it was for my grandfather when he was trying to get me to start loving the beautiful game of baseball instead of watching how long I could balance on my tippy toes.

For example, just before I left for spring training in 2022, my son's team—which I helped coach—had a practice where all we did was go to the batting cages. Sounds like a blast, right? Well, I look over and there is a good chunk of the team—mostly the Johnny-No-Pay-Attentions—all corralled in one cage, just yapping away. In the middle was my son.

"Knox," I said, "what are you doing over there?"

He said: "Dad, I can't help it. All they want to talk about is *Fortnite* and the color of their skin."

I told him, "First of all, don't rat out your friends. Second, be a leader and get them to focus." (The friends—not the dads—have to be the ones suggesting that it's cool to actually pay attention.)

Sure, we might get mad and we might put the team in time-out, but I'm under no illusion that either of those things will make these kids fall in love with baseball. We have to embrace what they're embracing, while erring on the side of rewarding (gummy bears and dollar bills can go a long way with six-year-olds, I've found). And I'm not going to get mad at kids for doing *Fortnite* dances in between drills. Will I be mad if the whole left side of the infield is doing it during a game, or while we're trying to teach them what a cutoff man does? Sure. But coaches and parents have to adjust. This can't be a my-way-or-the-highway mentality anymore. We simply have to start getting our heads around the fact that the old-school approach will not lead anybody to this game.

Go with the flow. Adjust. Feel it out. Move. Move. Move. That's what a good coach for these kids should be prioritizing.

The "We're going to do this until we get it right!" frame of mind is so stupid. How does that make any sense? We have to stimulate kids in the same way video games do. That's the world we're living in, and the sooner we realize it, the faster we're going to crack this baseball appreciation code.

Here is the simple truth: If the video game *Fortnite* wanted to take over the world right now, it could. If a message were inserted in that thing that suggested everyone should burn down everyone's house, all we would be seeing is a sea of flames. This is our reality right now. Relaying the art of moving a runner along with fewer than two outs is oftentimes going to have to wait. That time will come, but maybe just not in the manner we envisioned when mapping out our kids' journey to baseball greatness.

We also have to fight the temptation to force-feed the game on teenage kids. Their brains are developing in ways we adults can't fathom—even as hard as we try to think back on our own junior high and high school days. If we teach these kids the wrong way, it can not only push them away from baseball, it can be life-changing in so many ways.

Warning: You can start with a great kid who is allowed to become just an okay kid. That okay kid can then become a bad kid, and that bad kid can become something much worse.

Fun and encouragement have to stay at the top of our lists. We have to remember that while we are obsessing over having this game take root, these kids are fending off the pitfalls of bullying, puberty, and those first girlfriends or boyfriends. Everything leading to high school is end-of-the-world stuff.

Baseball should be part of the solution, not another part of the problem.

Up until 2020, it seemed like we might be righting the ship a bit when it came to convincing youngsters that baseball was worth their while. According to the Aspen Institute, the percentage of kids ages six through twelve who participated in baseball on a regular basis rose from 13.6 in 2018 to 14.4 a year later.

And as for the older ones—ages thirteen to seventeen—back in 2008, the percentage of consistent participation was 8.2, with the percentage jumping to 10.4 eleven years later.

The point is that the game was showing signs of life for the next generations.

Then came the pandemic and all that momentum hit a serious COVID-induced roadblock. The numbers in 2020 for both the six-to-twelve-year-olds and the thirteen-to-seventeen-year-olds dropped by around 2 percent in each category. All those reminders of how great this game is were overtaken by the ease of quarantine-necessitated video games.

The challenge that screen time presented was tough enough before, but now it was clear baseball had to work harder than ever. I'm here for the grind.

I know how easy it is to drift away from baseball, and I also realize how important it is to come back.

I still remember leaving.

By the time I got to junior high, I had no idea what a job felt like, but I imagined it was similar to what baseball was representing. The game I was really, really, really good at was no longer fun.

The grind of it all had simply overcome whatever joy initially led me to the diamond. That might seem odd for an eleven-year-old, but it was what it was. The practices. The driving around. The entire package that came with being a good baseball player had just worn me out. It's a feeling I'm sure isn't exclusive to me, with that travel ball lifestyle only intensifying by the day, but even back then this sort of burnout was a very real thing.

A sign that maybe my arms weren't wrapped all the way around baseball was the companion I carried to every practice and every road game—my skateboard.

I loved skateboarding more than I loved the game everybody was telling me should be my be-all and end-all. If there was a break in between practices, I would skateboard. Time in the middle of games? I'm jumping on my board. Baseball. Baseball. Baseball. That's what the world was throwing at me. But thanks in large part to kickflips, I found myself dodging opportunities to keep up with the best of the best in baseball, prioritizing those moments on the neighborhood ramp.

A few years ago, iconic pitcher Roger Clemens told a bunch of broadcasters that the one pitcher he was looking forward to watching that night was me. Some of those who heard the Rocket's proclamation breathlessly ran down to the field to tell me.

"That's nice," I responded, clearly dousing their excitement. Didn't I comprehend? This was Roger Clemens singling out me—Joe Kelly—from every other player. "You have to understand," I said in an attempt to clarify my reaction, "I wasn't watching baseball or Roger Clemens growing up. I was skateboarding."

At least for that window, during those all-important preteen years, that was dead-on. Bob Burnquist. Tony Hawk. Chad Muska. Those were my guys. I honestly can't remember watching a nine-inning baseball game until I had to start playing in them. So, Roger Clemens? Not on my radar.

And it was that reality that helped me definitively put baseball in my rearview mirror heading into high school. For me, it was simple: Baseball wasn't fun anymore, and other things were, like playing other sports with my brothers, getting into video games, and, of course, skateboarding. Fortunately, my parents—despite being divorced—found themselves on the same page and didn't push back, simply reading the room when it came to what their son wanted to do at what was a pretty important age. (What a novel concept.)

I look back in amazement at my mother, Andrea. I know I'm not alone in expressing admiration for a parent. They are the ones who sit on the hills, ward off the elements, and have to weather the small talk of fellow parents who aren't quite as grounded. And they are our rides. My mom did all of that for me and my three siblings. All the while, she somehow kept my situation in proper perspective, which allowed me to find my way.

The eye-rolling instead came from everywhere else.

Other parents. My friends. They couldn't get their heads around why somebody with all this God-given talent, who was getting to perform with the best of the bunch in his age group, was pushing it all aside to hang out with some skateboard punks. What they saw was me blowing kids away, always showing up on time to every practice and every game and seemingly having a good time while doing it all. What they didn't witness was my breaking down in tears because I had to leave my brother's birthday party and go play a game I really had lost interest in.

I can now look back and scream from the mountaintops: Taking a break from baseball was the best decision I ever made and absolutely allowed for my current relationship with the sport. To this day I peer back to that time as a fun time, an important time.

I would love to tell you the great game of baseball lured me back with all of the positives I find myself currently screaming about, but that simply wasn't the case. I just missed hanging out with my baseball-playing friends. I guess it's not all that different from a big-league player calling it quits and then attempting some sort of comeback, not because he wants to add to his Baseball-Reference.com page, but because duplicating that sense of brotherhood in real life isn't really an option.

So, I did go back. And when I did, I was a better player and a better person. And, oh yeah, I liked baseball a whole lot more.

I looked forward to the car rides. I looked forward to the practices. And I definitely looked forward to the games.

That was my crossroads. Eleven years old. Nowadays, such a fork in the road is being presented much earlier. In my opinion, it's too early.

Kids are being asked to define themselves at such a young age, being pushed into sports specialization by parents and coaches who fear falling behind. That's insane to me.

It is all a product of competition, and the opportunity for people to make a shit-ton of money. Complexes and fields are popping up all over the place, with parents more than happy to plop down wads of cash to fill them up. I know. I'm living through it now with my son. It has always been crazy competitive where I grew up and still live, Southern California, but the whole baseball-player-or-bust mentality has reached another level. Travel to games. Rent out practice time. Put on showcases. It's become a $15 billion industry in this country. That's one-five-billion.

It's hard for parents; I get it. Sure, some of it is the always-uncomfortable urge to live vicariously through the athletic successes of their children. But I do believe at the heart of it is the quest for the best when it comes to the kids. Who doesn't like seeing their offspring be successful at something? It's amazing.

It's been said over and over, but there is no handbook for how to raise a child, and there certainly isn't a blueprint for molding a Major League Baseball player. Just look at me.

But one simple part of the equation that parents can probably frame and put on their wall is this: Read the room.

If your kid shows an interest in getting a hoop for the backyard, sign them up for basketball. See them start imitating NFL players, maybe look at jumping onto a Pop Warner team. Or even if it has nothing to do with athletics at all, let them find the sweet spot when it comes to their interests. Heck, maybe baseball might be the one thing that emerges as the best of the bunch. It did for me, and you know why? Because my parents allowed for such an evolution to take place.

Parents these days are missing this very important perspective. And it's not just with regard to baseball. They are missing the little things. The hints. The clues. For me, it was dragging around a skateboard. These days, adults are way too concerned with keeping up with the Joneses instead of keeping an open mind until that fork in the road finally presents itself.

A big problem when it comes to the fanaticism of pushing sports on these kids is how often the parents—and young athletes—are reminded what they're up against. Thank you, Instagram. Thank you, Twitter. Thank you, Snapchat. "You want to go swimming with your friends? Forget it. I just watched a video of a seven-year-old who hit four home runs in a row! You need to practice!"

It's all smacking us in the face and simply not letting nature take its course. I'm in the middle of it, fighting off all those temptations to immediately attach superstar status to my kids. Every time that urge comes over me, I remember carrying around that skateboard to those practices. I also look around and see how fast all these youngsters are being asked to grow up, and it's not good. If we keep going down this road, we're going to regret it as parents, and the kids themselves will be the victims.

I was watching *Star Wars* the other day, and it was one of those things where Luke Skywalker wants to become a Jedi, and everybody knows he will probably become a Jedi. But Obi-Wan Kenobi knows he has to slow-play it and make sure the path is the proper one. He let the boy be the boy. Let's learn from Obi-Wan.

And, believe me, nobody said it was easy.

These kids are being bombarded with stuff I couldn't have imagined, distracting them from finding the purity in what could end up being their life's passion. You think I was being pulled to and fro by the amount of YouTube or video game offerings these young people are? Not a chance. And then you get into having to deal with the real-world ugliness of war and such conveyed to these kids on a minute-by-minute basis. They are already being forced into a world they don't belong in. Kids have to be allowed to be kids, and right now that is becoming less of an option.

What happened to simply figuring out how to calculate a batting average?

It's a helpless feeling because there is only so much we can reel in with social media consistently starting it back up, just when we thought the stream of chaos was slowing down. Maybe this is where baseball can help.

Sometimes we have to make the extra effort to allow this great sport to slow things down and appreciate the important stuff. Then there are the moments when it slaps us across the face. And sometimes those wake-up calls are the simplest and purest images a game can present.

Like, for instance, a simple trip around the bases.

Ninety feet of dirt will go a long way to simplify what has become a way-too-complicated world. The run to first, and then turning the corner into the realization that you get to touch at least one more base. Now you're rounding second and heading to the last stop before the ultimate endpoint. And then there is that last stretch, one where all you can think about is the accomplishment that comes with making baseball's ultimate journey. Anybody who has played the game understands these emotions.

Now, remember what it was like to take off on this jaunt as a kid. Or, better yet, watch the face of any youngster who navigates these 360 feet.

Back in the midst of some June doldrums during the 2022 season, both our White Sox team and the Orioles got a shock to the system when soaking in the joy of a seven-year-old named Beau Dowling. Beau is a cancer patient whose wish was to swing for the fences at the home park of his White Sox, and then simply run around the bases. This bravest of young men, who had already experienced three lifetimes of adversity, just wanted to complete this hallowed circle.

No crying in baseball? Good luck with that.

Say what you want about baseball, there is no other sport that fixes what ails someone thanks to such simple acts. Personally, I make sure to take advantage of the blessing every time the club opens up the field for families after Sunday home games. That's when my own six-year-old gets his chance to soak in the joy that a baseball diamond can deliver, while I sit back and remember why we care so much.

Long plane rides. Two hours of sleep. Aches and pains. Man, I'm playing a kid's game. One glance over to Knox experiencing the joy that I always hoped baseball would bring him reminds me of that every single time.

Let the kids play, and let the rest of us revel in it. When it comes to resuscitating baseball, that's a good place to start.

CHAPTER NINE

AN OPEN LETTER TO MY KIDS

K nox. Crue. Blake.

Those three little words (your names) are the best three words I have said since I told your mother "I love you" for the first time.

I have been blessed to play a kid's game for a living the past eleven years of my life. I shared the first few years of my career with just your mom by my side. The next few years I shared with my best friend, Knox. (Don't worry, Crue and Blake, you guys weren't thought of yet.) Now, the past two years I have spent with my beautiful daughter, Blake, and my gorgeous baby boy, Crue. What I thought I knew of this world before you three knuckleheads were in my life has completely changed.

What I thought about a silly game with a stick and a ball before you guys were born has completely changed. The lessons you get as a Major League Baseball player come in many shapes and sizes. I used to think that all that mattered was how well I performed in front of thousands of people. I thought that was the only thing that counted. Once I had you three, all of that went down the drain. And, honestly, you guys made me a better person, a better husband, and a better teammate.

Oh, yeah. You also made me a better baseball player.

I will never take for granted any and every moment we spend together on this planet called Earth. The shittiest days I have ever had at work become the easiest once I leave the field and head home. Not because I forget what I had done earlier in the day or night, like blowing a lead at the end of a game to an archrival, but because I know that what really matters in the world is your mom and the three sweet little faces I get to come home to and kiss.

Don't get me wrong. Losing freaking sucks. Losing sucks even more when you are the one who blows it. If you guys are anything like your mom and me, you will eventually know what it feels like to win and to lose. But here is the thing: It took me twenty-eight years to understand that sports are not what define you as a human being. What defines you are your beliefs, your family, and your friends. A silly game doesn't define who you are.

Now, I'm going to try to share some wisdom with you three. Obviously, once you all can read, you will have a chance to come back and soak in what I wish for you guys instead of hearing what I have to say. (Sometimes it's better to read anyway, because the barking from your parents can get a little tiresome. Also, believe it or not, I don't always communicate my thoughts or feelings as well as I should.)

I could write for days on end about all the things I hope the future of competition brings for you guys, but that would defeat the purpose since you guys are children, and according to the stats, I'm about to lose your focus in the next few minutes. So, let me try my best and keep it simple. I have some promises from me to you all that I would like to share.

Here we go . . .

—Children, I promise to let you be a kid as long as possible. (But once you are an adult, you will be treated as one.)

—I promise to keep my mouth shut when your coaches are talking to you. (But when your coaches are done helping, I can promise to also show you what I know.)

—I promise to never get on your asses for playing a bad game. (But trust me, I know how hard it is.) I do promise, however, to definitely get on your asses for moping or lack of effort. Just play hard.

—I promise to always be available for "catch," shooting hoops, extra passes, or shots on goal even if I am dead tired.

—I promise to never yell in the stands or bleachers. I can't promise your mom doing the same.

—I promise your mom will always have the best snacks and treats when it's our turn to bring them after games.

—I promise to be the best coach in anything you guys decide you want to do, and if somehow I'm not the best coach or don't know what I'm talking about, then I will find the best one around.

—I promise to be your father first in all aspects of life.

—I promise to be proud of you.

—I promise to be stern when you need it and soft when you need a shoulder to cry on.

—I promise always to be transparent.

—I promise always to listen.

—I promise to kiss you on the cheek for the rest of your lives.

—I promise to be the best dad I can possibly be.

—I promise to love you all for the rest of my life.

Knox, Crue, and Blake: Play hard. Play fast. Play fierce. Play to win, damn it. But most of all, play to have fun! Whatever you choose to play, have freaking fun! And if you choose not to play sports anymore or ever even get into sports, I promise to never force you to play or give you guilt for not playing. Not everyone was made to play sports, and that's okay, too. But whatever you choose to do, I promise you better work your damn asses off. Children, remember this, in all aspects of life: "Tough nuts, kick butts."

Love, Dad

CHAPTER TEN

DON'T TAKE MY WORD FOR IT

I'm just one guy.

There will be some who suggest that anyone who has the audacity to tackle the very complicated existence that is baseball should treat the endeavor like a scientific dissertation.

Surely one big-league ballplayer whose post-professional baseball existence likely involves becoming an undercover narcotics agent or full-time dad—living a world away from anything to do with the National Baseball Hall of Fame or any other kind of ball-playing immortalization—can't speak to such complicated matters. Not enough facts. Not enough figures. Not enough success. Not enough examples. Not enough perspective.

Yes, I'm just one guy. But that's the beauty of this whole conversation about our damn near perfect game. When it comes to the conversation about baseball, everybody has a sweet spot. Stories. Opinions. Facts. Figures. Smiles. Tears. Lessons.

So, don't just take my word for it . . .

Mark Hoppus, Musician

Mark is one of the most interesting people I know, and not only because of his existence as the bassist and colead vocalist for the wildly popular group blink-182. He is not only an artist, he is a thinker, which is why the Southern Californian found himself ultimately infatuated with baseball.

So, I had no interest in baseball whatsoever until my late thirties. No interest at all. I thought it was boring. I thought the games took too long. I thought it took too long in between pitches. I didn't get it at all.

Then we had a friend who came to our house, and he was like, "Can we put on the Dodgers game?"

I immediately said: "Man, you're going to watch baseball? It's kind of boring."

And he responds, "Oh, no, you don't understand."

So, he starts breaking down the game for me. This is how the game has a rhythm. There are pitchers vs. batters. This is the whole thing with pitch counts. This is what it means when a hitter gets ahead in the count or falls behind in the count, and why that dictates what the pitcher throws.

I started understanding it all and realized baseball is the perfect game, because you can go to a game and, if you want, read a book—or analyze the whole scene—between pitches and still pay full attention to what is going on. I started getting it a lot better. Then I started getting into the history of the players. When was the last time this pitcher got that batter out? Who hit the grand slam off that guy? All of it. It just makes the game so much more interesting, and so, so beautiful.

I love watching baseball. It's awesome, in part because it's kind of always there. They play so many games, it's always there for you to take in. I love it all. I love going to games. I love listening to the commentators. I just think once you learn the rhythm of the game and know just a little bit about the players and a little bit about the history, it makes it so much more enjoyable.

And I tell you what, I would imagine being on a baseball team isn't all that different from being in a band. Everybody in a band does something different. They're doing their own thing, but they all work together as a unit, trying to do something beautiful. And, hopefully, when things are firing, you get it. For instance, we can be onstage and Travis Barker could be having an amazing night and I'm having an off night and the whole thing feels like it's falling apart. I will walk offstage and be like, "Fuck, that show was rough," and Travis will be like, "We had a great show!"

And then there are those times where everything just clicks and everything feels so effortless, those times you feel like you should just get out the way and let the music flow through you. For me the best nights are when I'm not even thinking about it and it is just happening to me. Those times I'm in as much awe as everybody else. I'm like, "Shit! I'm playing well tonight."

When I was young I certainly had no idea I would ultimately fall in love with baseball. I just wanted to play music. And when I got to high school, I started listening to bands I liked on my own. When I heard "Silly Girl" by The Descendents, that changed my whole world forever and ever.

I had been playing bass and learning my instruments, but then I heard that and I immediately thought: *That's what I want to do. That's the sound I didn't know I needed in my life that completes me.* This was part of me that I didn't know was there until I heard that music. After that, all I wanted to do was play in a band and play bass guitar. Before that, I never wanted to play guitar. I never wanted to solo. I never wanted anything like that. I just wanted to be a bassist because I love what the bass does in music. It's the foundation. It's the bridge between the rhythm and the melody. It ties in with the melody because it lays the foundation for chord progressions that the guitarist and the vocalists go over and do all the magic and get all the shine. The bass is the foundation of all of that. I love that.

It's not unlike baseball and how you don't notice how important the little things are like that until they're not there.

Another similarity between living in a group and being on a baseball team is how you have to interact with one another. I think my strength in Blink is that I don't need to control everything, but I need to know everything. That's just my personality. I don't have to tell Tom to do something or tell Travis to do something, but I need to know what all the pieces are doing. So, my place in Blink, and in music in general, is to be very foundational. I try to pull everything back to the center and keep everything organized. I would imagine a baseball clubhouse has those sorts of guys as well.

This is the balance of our group. When Tom has these big giant visions and he wants to do these soaring melodies and he wants to go do stadiums and explore musically and do all kinds of stuff, I'm always trying to pull him back toward, "Okay, how does this make any sense in the song?

How can we make this concise? How can we make this work all together?" That's what I do, and that's just me feeling the need to understand everything. And maybe that's one of the reasons I love baseball. There is so much to understand and organize.

Nowadays, so many people are talking about changing the games and rule changes and things like that. I just love baseball so much I can't really think of things I would want to change. Sure, there are nitpicky things. A pitch clock. Robo-umpires. I don't think like that. Don't think those things help or hinder the game one way or another. I just think baseball is so beautiful.

Just the other night, there was something that went viral where a dude hits a home run to this guy, and the guy gives the ball to a little kid and the kid goes crazy. Then a few hours later, another guy hits a home run, the kid gets it and gives it to the guy that caught the first ball. It's crazy. I love that stuff.

It's a kind sport. It's a beautiful sport. It is intense. And it's super-American. I just know that over the last fifteen years, I have really come to appreciate it.

Dennis Eckersley, Hall of Famer

Eck is a Hall of Fame relief pitcher whose career epitomized the ups, downs, adversity, and triumphs that baseball can represent. Known for his fiery approach on the mound, Dennis morphed from a good-but-not-great starting pitcher into one of the best relief pitchers in the history of the game. He never shied away from the tough conversations and the tough moments—including what became an iconic moment in baseball when Kirk Gibson took him deep to win Game 1 of the 1988 World Series. Four years later, he would win both the Cy Young and American League MVP. There are few people in this game who have ridden the roller coaster that is big-league baseball like Eck, whose passion for the game has never been hard to uncover.

Being emotional. You are or you aren't. How do you teach someone not to be emotional? "Stop that!" It doesn't happen. If anything, I was encouraged. Harvey Haddix was my first pitching coach in the big leagues. I remember I was really demonstrative and he didn't say anything, and neither did my manager, Frank Robinson. They liked it. I remember I had a couple of bad games, and Harvey would come out and say, "Where is that emotion?"

But, man, I was beat up. He was like, "Bring it!" That's what he thought made me good, but I never thought twice about it.

But I can tell you, there is nothing like it. Baseball brings that out. Everybody wants to be good and have that kind of control over their situation. I mean, you're good at something. You're really, really good at something! It's a gift.

It was a feeling I started having when I was about ten or twelve years old, knowing that you're better than everyone else. That's a good feeling. There's one thing to have those emotions when you're dominant, but it's quite something else when the real pressure comes. That didn't come for me for a long time, until I was collecting paychecks. It was right away in pro ball, when I went to play in the California League. That was a tough league for a seventeen-year-old. It was a rude awakening. It got my attention real quick, knowing I couldn't just bring it and that I was actually going to have to learn how to pitch. That's when it's nut-cutting time. That's when guys fall by the wayside.

I thought the hard part was trying to catch up to my older brother, Wally, and his friends when I was a kid. Nope. It's a vicious cycle. You finally become dominant, but then comes the expectations. And then when you fail after finally getting those expectations, it's devastating.

It's why there is nothing like being a pitcher. This is what delivers the feelings that life is built on.

You have the ball in your hand and that's the most important person on the field. That's emotional in itself. You have complete control. Then you have those individual moments that make you remember that reality.

What's weird is that those instances that should allow for all that bottled euphoria are hard to really soak in. Looking back, I didn't really enjoy those moments because there was always doubt hanging around. Lurking.

The best is when you're a starting pitcher, you pitch a complete game and you have five days to gloat. But the relief pitching thing? "Yeah!" It can be awesome. There is that high of pitching in the ninth inning. That's really high. How can you not be emotional in those situations? But then you get to your locker, go home, and realize you have to do it again the next day. It's a short blast. You just can't sustain that emotion, although you sure wish you could.

I remember I first started relieving twelve years into my major league career. Oh my God! I was flying. As long as I had been in the big leagues, I had never had that feeling. I had done it a few times when I was younger, but not like this, where it was my job. I was Superman. That's a shot in the arm, man, if you're ready. It's a great feeling. But the opposite side of that is, wow . . .

Well, that came with the Kirk Gibson home run.

Again, that was not a whole lot different than those other relief-pitching bursts of emotion. The sting actually wasn't that bad from the Gibson thing. The offseason allowed me to have six months of just thinking about the next game. "Let's go!"

But whether it's the World Series or just another game, there's nothing like that feeling of the highs and lows. If you lived with me, you would know that every time I gave it up, I lived it hard, especially as a reliever. It's tough and, I have to be honest, it gets to you after a while.

Fortunately, the good times are there to help balance things out a bit. For instance, I still hold on to that feeling of that first game of the '88 playoffs when we were playing the Red Sox at Fenway Park. Wade Boggs was up with two on, and I punched him out on three pitches. Wade Boggs! That was a moment. If he doesn't punch out, he's going to hit that left field wall just to stay in shape. But I punched him out. I remember it like it was yesterday. He took one. I sunk one. And then I threw it right fucking by him. Yes! That was a hell of a moment.

That's what I'm talking about. How can you not think baseball is all about emotion?

Rob Friedman, Pitching Ninja

Rob exemplifies the new age of both baseball fan and player. Through his brand, Pitching Ninja, and the videos and analyses it has been built on, he has constructed an unmatched following in the world of baseball. Major leaguers and television networks turn to Rob for the kind of conversation that has helped not only build his mission, but baseball fandom as a whole.

Simply put, Pitching Ninja represents part of the solution when it comes to the continued building of baseball.

As a kid, I was always a big fan. It was one of those things where you want to grow up to be a baseball player back in the day. But it really took having my own kid and trying to explain sports, and really everything else, through baseball that made me fall back in love with it.

I had played on and off through high school, but I wasn't very good. I tried. My parents were both teachers and really prioritized academics. Sports was a thing, but it wasn't a huge thing for me. But deep down I still always wanted to play baseball, so I started studying it. That was awesome.

The internet started blowing up and so did video analysis, allowing me to take part in the sport in a completely different way while teaching it to the next generation. I was able to give to people what I would have wanted back when I was falling in love with baseball.

When my son was growing up, we had season tickets to the Braves with Greg Maddux and Tom Glavine and all those guys pitching. There wasn't a better time to be a baseball fan and, more specifically, a fan of pitching in that world. It made my son want to be like a combination of Chipper Jones and Barry Bonds all at the same time. Stuff like that.

Then we came to really understand that baseball is made to be dissected in so many different ways.

You can love it as a sport, especially if you're good at it. But people also like it because they're into analytics and math, because baseball is very much a math-oriented sport.

It's a very one-on-one competition sport, like a cross between boxing and chess. You're trying to beat the hitter. The hitter is trying to beat the pitcher. Then you have the chess aspects of it, which are the analytics with all the sequencing.

My realization and involvement in all of this just kind of happened over time. What I did was start learning from message boards. All these conversations would be taking place with guys who ended up being successful in the baseball world. We used to bounce ideas off each other, coming from different areas of expertise. I thought: *Hey, I'm coaching. What I want to do is pass the game on to the next generation because I'm not going to coach forever, right?* I had this unique access to people, and I had been successful in internet software, so I was able to buy like every single training aid you could possibly have. I didn't want everybody else to have to do what I did.

I figured I could help them learn from me, helping people who maybe didn't have the money or the ability to take lessons, or just wanted to ask their coach different questions to get more information. That's all I tried to do is share all of that. Then more and more people started saying, "This is kind of cool." And then I had pro guys reach out to me for advice. It just kept blowing up more and more. Certainly more than I ever intended.

All of a sudden I'm having a debate with legendary closer Billy Wagner over Randy Johnson's mechanics on Twitter. He was really interested because they had pitched together.

Billy said, "You know, Randy used his lower half really well."

I was like, "He really didn't." And I showed him videos.

He was like, "Oh my God, he didn't!" And he played on the same team as him.

I'm just amazed every day at every direction all the conversations have taken off in. All of it has been eye-opening, including when I got my Twitter account suspended.

The suspension came because I was sharing videos, and Major League Baseball didn't allow you to do that. They contacted me and I just thought, *Oh, well, either I'm never going to tweet again, which is fine because it would give me more time, or they're going to feel pressure and want me to do it.*

Sure enough they contacted me again after that and said: "We love what you do. We just want to be more official. Would you like to be a contractor with us?"

I'm like, "Sure. Absolutely!"

Listen, I'm just passing on my love of the game. I think they thought that because they owned the content and people shared it that somehow it was going to make people not watch the games. Instead, people watch more games, without a doubt, because of social media sharing and everyone's love for the game. It has to be organic, because if MLB is just doing it, they are going to be viewed as self-serving and somewhat out of touch with the average fan. There are so many different ways to lift the game up, and I think they realize that now. But it took a while.

It's all been crazy, like Yu Darvish asking me for advice on Shane Bieber's knuckle-curve over DM. And there have been a lot of those types of moments. Every time an announcer says the word "Airbender" when talking about Devin Williams's changeup. Every time someone uses the term "sword." To see all this influence that a dude with a computer, who wasn't any good at baseball, has is incredible to me. I swear it never gets old.

And these pitches just keep getting more amazing. Things like Devin Williams's changeup. Emmanuel Case throwing 101- or 102-mile-an-hour cutters is never going to get old for me. It just won't. Jhoan Durán's slinker is kind of ridiculous because, let's face it, a 101 mph off-speed pitch is kind of insane. Clay Holmes, watching his sinker. There are just so many different folks. And what we're doing is uncovering new ways to make the ball move. You would have to think we've tapped everything over a hundred-something years, but we're still figuring out new ways that seams make the ball move that had never been figured out before. And it's all happening right before our eyes.

A guy like Corey Kluber bringing his whirly slider to the Yankees and all of a sudden Michael King learns it and then the whole staff ends up learning it. That kind of thing has such a huge effect on the game, because people end up wondering why that pitch moves so much, and they couldn't figure it out through traditional models. Why? Because all the traditional models are missing one thing, and that was the weight caused by the seams to make the ball move differently. Pitchers don't even know why it's happening, but it's science that is making it happen. Some care. Some don't. But we do know the ball is moving as it has never moved before.

Now, for baseball's sake, the challenge is explaining what's actually going on without either talking down to them, talking over their heads, or saying the game was better back in my day. So, I think it's important to be able to explain it through video, through words, and whatever is going to get through to the fan. Currently, you do have a generation of announcers who played the game, but they're always yearning for the days back when they played and not appreciating how today's game incorporates so much. It's science. It's math. It's athleticism. It's training. It's the mental game. It's all of this, and we're trying to make people see that.

And we also have to remember that while there is a science to it, at the end of the day, it's people competing to it. Maybe if we tell fans this in a different way, so that we're not speechifying or talking at them. If we just say, "Hey, this is what you might expect." And, "This is really cool, so watch . . ." Maybe that will give them some excitement about it.

If everybody acts like they've been there before and stuff isn't exciting and blah, blah, blah, then fans aren't going to be excited. If you act like this is the coolest crap ever, then fans will appreciate it. A lot of people love the game because of analytics, which is cool and okay. But a lot of people watch the game, and they don't want a math class. They don't want words they don't understand. And it's great to have them.

But you can also say, "Wouldn't it be cool if we could just measure how fast the ball left the bat, at what angle, and how many stadiums that would have been a hit in?" Well, that's Expected Batting Average (xBA) and Expected Slugging Percentage (xSLG). People don't use those terms, but if you explain them in detail and say, "This is why this is important," then you might get people saying, "Oh, I get it." But we end up talking at them instead of talking to them.

Let's start talking to them, because I know this: Baseball is always a great conversation.

Bo Bichette, All-Star Shortstop

Bo is not only one of Major League Baseball's best young stars, playing shortstop for one of baseball's most exciting teams, the Blue Jays, but he has reached these heights as the son of a former major leaguer, Dante Bichette. Dante made the All-Star team four times during a fourteen-year career, with Bo being brought into the world four years before Dante ultimately called it quits as a member of the Red Sox. But just because Bo's father was a big leaguer, that doesn't mean he was spared the roller coaster that kids can ride when it comes to defining their love for the game.

I think my parents did a good job of allowing me to choose what I wanted to do. Growing up, actually, my dad wanted me to be a tennis player. So, I definitely found the love for baseball on my own. There was no doubt that having my dad as a big-league ballplayer gave me a head start on everybody, understanding what major leaguers go through and already being so engaged in the sport. Now that I'm here, I can understand what he was talking about. But I didn't always.

I actually quit the game when I was young, probably around eleven years old. Basically, my dad was constantly teaching me what it took to get here. But at that time I was like, "I don't want to work that hard." So I stopped for a little bit.

I enjoyed playing baseball, but I was playing a lot of tennis, too. I loved it, and to this day Rafael Nadal is my favorite athlete. I needed that time off. It was around the time when my dad became hitting coach of the Rockies that I started getting back into it. Just being around the guys and the game. Then came high school, and my parents told me I had to pick one of the two, and for me it became a no-brainer.

After that time away, I knew I would be happy giving everything I could to baseball, where I just couldn't do the same with tennis. Sometimes it takes some time to pick your passion, and that was the case with me. The major leaguers were the ones I looked up to, walking in the clubhouse when my dad was playing. Nomar Garciaparra, for instance, was the guy. I remember in kindergarten writing a book about him—as much as a kindergartener can—talking about how he was my favorite athlete. And while I didn't really have posters, I had those Fathead images (larger-than-life wall decals). David Ortiz. Jacoby Ellsbury. Almost all Red Sox. I was into it.

The break was important for me, but I understand that the more you put into one thing the better you are going to be. And nowadays kids are being pushed toward trying to be a professional more than when I was coming up. It took me until I was in high school before I knew I wanted to play, but now you have kids who are playing year-round. I do feel it's important to have a balance.

I have also realized what a great game baseball is. It's an absolutely unbelievable sport, and there are so, so many unbelievably exciting players around the game. But I do believe one problem we're having is that we are making the game a bit too difficult to understand. Back when I was falling in love with baseball, everybody knew what a home run was, and everybody knew what an RBI was. Now we're being evaluated on OPS-plus and xFIP. Not to say those things aren't valuable tools, but it's become tougher for younger kids to understand and for parents to teach their kids.

I just think we need to get back to simplifying the game a bit for fans, because it's such a great game. People should understand that.

Rob Lowe, Actor

Over the last four decades, Rob has become one of the film and TV industry's most iconic actors, and one of its most visible sports fans. While he broke into the entertainment business as a fifteen-year-old, his introduction into all things baseball came well before that, growing up in Dayton, Ohio, before moving to Malibu, California. Whether it was through those early years rooting for the Reds, or as one of the Dodgers' most famous fans, it's not hard to decipher the impact baseball has left on the former Pony Leaguer.

I fell in love with baseball through the Big Red Machine (the Cincinnati Reds) in the seventies. I grew up in Dayton, Ohio, and Al Michaels was the voice of the Reds. I listened to all the games as a kid, went to Riverfront Stadium, and was just a fanatic for that run, which I still think is probably the greatest lineup ever. Got to be. So I came into baseball spoiled. My team was the best team that ever lived, that a fan ever watched.

Pete Rose, for instance, only cared about winning. One of the greatest moments in my life was when he was managing the Reds and I was at Dodger Stadium to watch. I had really good seats. He came out to make a pitching change. But what I realized was that he came out to make a pitching change just so he could find where I was sitting and motion to me, "I'll call you!" He's a good dude. That was a great moment.

I have so many great baseball memories. I've been so lucky and blessed. I was there for Kirk Gibson's home run. I was there in person. We were all leaving. I was walking out of the stadium, sort of walking backward up the steps. Then I was there for the eighteen-inning game. I stayed for the whole thing because it was the "Gibson Lesson." Never, ever, ever leave a game until it's over because if something like that happens you'll never forgive yourself. I knew people who left right before Max Muncy hit that home run. They stayed for seventeen innings and the eighteenth was too much. That was the bridge too far. If they waited just ten minutes, they would have seen one of the great moments in Dodgers history.

I sat directly behind home plate for Doc Gooden in that rookie year. I have never seen anybody pitch like that to this day. Gooden that first year was just insane. He was literally unhittable. He had these matchups with Pedro Guerrero that were just legendary.

I came up at a great time in baseball. They were true characters. Those were amazing times.

I remember sitting with Tommy Lasorda watching a game, and I forget what the other team was doing but they were being dicks. I'm like, "Tommy, in your day, how quickly would you have thrown at those guys?"

He just said, "I'll tell you something, if they wouldn't have thrown at them on their own, I would have made them."

If a guy hits a ball too hard, and he's up again, I'm sorry . . . It's just unbelievable people won't do it. There's that great story: When Gibson came to the Dodgers, they had been on the threshold but never got over it. In spring training they filled his mitt up with whipped cream and everybody thought it was hilarious. But he went just fucking ape-shit on them. That attitude . . . I think the Dodgers historically need a badass because we're SoCal, easygoing. I'm always looking to see who is going to be the asshole on our Dodgers team.

It reminds everybody why they fell in love with the game when they were kids and they were your buddies, and your brothers and you hung out and it wasn't a business. It's awesome.

So many memories . . . I got to watch a game sitting next to Vin Scully and it was the year they were debating whether to extend the netting. He's talking about how a fan got killed in Dodger Stadium in the late sixties by a line-drive. I'm like, "No way. I would have heard about it."

Then he just went and explained the whole thing and it was like I turned the radio on. "It was a doubleheader in the middle of August. A young man had made his way to the stadium from Long Beach and he took a foul ball off the bat of Manny Mota. He left the stands to a standing ovation but died on the way to the hospital." There have been a lot of great ones, but Vin is the greatest.

Just to have favorites that you latch onto forever is such a huge part of baseball. My favorite player, for instance, has to be somebody off the Big Red Machine. It's like your first favorite song as a kid. You have favorite songs as an adult but it never quite matches what you listened to when you were a teenager.

Every time you walk into that ballpark. Every time you see that one player, witness that one play. These are the kinds of emotions no other sport can offer.

Torey Krug, Hockey Player

Torey came into the National Hockey League exactly ten weeks before I made my debut in Major League Baseball, also falling in love with his other sport—baseball—around the same time I was first being introduced to the game. We both lived the life of professional athletes in Boston for the majority of our careers, with Torey playing for the Bruins before reaping the rewards of free agency with a seven-year contract to play in the place I started, St. Louis. Hockey might have taken over his life, but his love for baseball has remained a constant. Want proof? He named his dog "Fenway" after my former home ballpark with the Red Sox.

I remember pretty clearly that one time when a first baseman got in my way on the base paths. Let's just say I let it be known he better get out of my way. I was a thirteen-year-old hockey player who just loved baseball, and I wasn't about to separate the two.

I was always a smaller kid, always trying to prove people wrong. Even to this day, I'm still proving people wrong. I have this pride that doesn't always serve me well because I want to show everyone I can play with the bigger guys and be more physical than bigger guys. For me, that was something that always showed up. I was always reaching to prove people wrong and had this intensity about myself. That's what made me good at hockey, and that's also what made me good at baseball.

In both sports emotions run high. I spent a lot of time on the mound in my younger years, and I was able to throw pretty hard at a young age and there was a little bit of an intimidation factor to some of the batters at the time. To me, too, if a kid clobbered the ball and he got on base, that next couple of batters I was reaching back and throwing as hard as I could because I was really upset. If a guy was crowding the plate, I would do my best to push him back even at a young age. I think that was just the hockey instincts coming out. You can take things into your own hands in baseball, so that was my way of combining the two. It's why I fell in love with the game.

It began as soon as I could get up and play catch in the yard with my brothers. I watched them play. As soon as I could play I was right in the mix. Believe or not, for a while I loved baseball just as much if not more than hockey. There was nothing like playing catch in the yard with my brothers and my dad. Spending time outside. Times are a little bit different these days with social media and technology, but back then you were outside all day long. All you needed was a ball, a bat, and a couple of gloves, and if you didn't have that, just a Wiffle Ball would do. Being outside with my brothers every day in the summer brought me under baseball's spell.

I was thrown onto skates as soon as I could walk. I was always around the rink, 24/7, at my brothers' games. My dad was a coach in the Detroit area. That was very well known. I loved hockey immediately. But as I became more competitive at baseball, I wanted to pursue it, and if I'd been a little better I might have. But at some point you run out of time. My hockey coaches didn't like that I would be missing time for baseball. The two schedules just stopped working together. I had to choose.

I miss those days. Catcher. Shortstop. And especially pitching. I just loved the competitive side of it all.

The emotion of it all was there for me as a fan, too. My team, do or die, was the Tigers. In 2002, they had 106 losses. The next year, 119. It didn't matter. I was all in. The minute I walked into Comerica Park as a kid, I was hooked. There is just something magic about entering a big-league ballpark for the first time. And then, a few years later, when the Tigers actually made it to the World Series, emotions were sky high. Watching those big hits and home runs. That was the payoff.

The feel of the park. It's one of things baseball delivers that pretty much no other sport can.

Then came Fenway Park. The best of the best.

When I was playing for the Bruins, I got a chance to become friends with some of the Red Sox (because that's what happens when you play in Boston). In my opinion, those are the greatest fans in the world. So, when I was presented with the opportunity to throw out the first pitch at Fenway, I almost lost my mind. There I was, meeting David Ortiz during batting practice, and he was standing outside the cage just asking me about my first name. What baseball kid couldn't cherish something like that? To this day, it is one of my coolest moments.

And then came the actual pitch. Pitching on those young baseball mounds in Michigan was one thing. Fenway? That was something completely different. There was one problem: I had just had shoulder surgery and the Bruins didn't want me to do it. I called the surgeon and said: "Look, this is a dream of mine. You have to let me do it! I promise I won't be stupid about it." Finally, he gave me the green light. That was the first obstacle.

The second? My nerves. Fortunately, Joe Kelly invited me to come down and play catch before I went out. That calmed me down a little. But, clearly, the bravado I had known as a pitcher wasn't anywhere to be found this time around. Eight other guys weren't relying on me, but my ego was. In the end, I think I did a pretty good job.

There are just so many things about baseball that offer those life-defining moments. I play hockey, but I never forget about baseball. That's what the sport does to you.

David Ross, Manager

Rossy is viewed as the ultimate player's manager, in large part because he wasn't a player all that long ago. And when he was playing and/or winning the World Series with the Red Sox and the Cubs, he was considered as close to a manager on the field as you're going to find. David has witnessed how baseball has changed when it comes to players, clubhouses, and approaches since he first came into the majors in 2002. There is perhaps nobody better to relay how it was, how it is, and where it is going.

Managing these days is definitely different. Looking at it from a player's perspective, nobody gets taken out at second and nobody gets run over at home plate. We're so conscious of pitch counts and taking care of bodies, more than ever before. That part of it has been heightened since I was a player. Back then it didn't matter how you felt, you had to figure it out. We just kind of rolled guys out there.

But what makes it fun is that it just feels like a younger game.

You see guys come up and they have a mindset that they would always make it here. I remember getting all the way to the big leagues and I was floored. I never thought in my wildest dreams I was going to make it to the major leagues. But they have the expectation that they will get there. And when they do, veterans are more on their side than ever before. When I first came up, you were made to feel like a rookie. Not anymore. And, you know what? That's a good thing.

You want these guys to feel at home, and when they do it's rewarding. Wilson Contreras, just the other day, did something that reminded me of that. The game was on the line and Chris Morel, a rookie, was up with a runner on third. The crowd is on its feet and you have this twenty-two-year-old in the batter's box. He swings at the first pitch in the dirt, and then he swings at the next one over his head. Wilson just whistles over to him and makes the motion to take a deep breath. Relax. The moment speeds up on you and you're trying harder than you should. You've just got to slow things down, which is what Wilson was taking the time to teach Chris in that moment. I love to see that interaction. It's just really cool.

As a manager, you have to create that kind of communication with everybody. I honestly don't know if I spoke to one of my managers until I was a couple of years in, and that was because they were telling me I was playing the next day. Now I will sit down with a guy and tell him where I'm putting him in the lineup and why, or I'll just talk to him about his family. Sometimes you have to desensitize yourself from that manager's chair a bit. I picture myself as a player now, or as an ex-player who's just trying to help out rather than this dictator that controls everything. You have to have reliability.

It's just different these days.

I was telling somebody the other day . . . We were struggling so somebody asked if I was going to go in and flip over the food table. I'm like, "No. That would just make everybody hungry. Right? We want guys to eat because it's a hard season." You just have to keep talking about the priorities when it comes to winning. You have to relate to these guys and feel where they're coming from. That's where I feel like I have a good handle on things.

I got to be part of two championship teams, but I also know what it's like to be released. There are so many different roles I have played in and played for so many different kinds of managers, so I think when I talk to these guys they can relate. I just try to tell my stories. If they start to suck, I can say, "Hey, let me tell you about my whole career of fifteen years stinking."

I think as a player the most I felt at home was playing for Terry Francona. Back in 2008, I got a chance to join a championship-caliber organization that was on its way to the playoffs and he just calls me in and says, "Hey, Rossy, we don't have a lot of plays and you can throw through to second base unless I tell you to eat it and we have a great group of guys. You're going to feel like family in two days, so just have fun. If you need anything, let me know." That was it. And then he would be on the bench early and I would go out there and listen to him and Dustin Pedroia shoot the breeze, or watch him play cards with guys and think that he just felt like he was one of the boys. That's how you have to be.

There are always going to be tough conversations when things get out of hand, or you have to sit somebody down or release someone. Stuff like that. Those are the hard parts of the job. But I also learned from Joe Maddon not to sweat the small stuff. We don't need to stress about the wardrobe on the plane, and if guys don't want to hit that day then let them make the decision not to hit that day. Batting practice is overrated sometimes. You need to know what's important to make them feel better. I'm going to pick my battles.

Things have definitely changed, however.

When you're talking about dressing or not taking BP, Bobby Cox would have had a really hard time with it. Bobby wanted us to wear collared shirts . . . at home. And we were in the National League East, going down to Miami with slacks and a collared shirt. Man, it was hot. But Bobby gave you so many other freedoms, like there was no team stretch, and you didn't hear much negative stuff from him other than he expected you to play hard, be prepared every day, and give me a good effort. At the end of the day, that's what you're trying to do. It really doesn't matter if we walk into the team hotel at four in the morning after a long road trip in board shorts and flip-flops. Nobody cares, right? I've learned that you just have to chill on some of that stuff because it just doesn't matter. Just put the focus on winning and the things you believe in that will build a winning atmosphere.

It all comes from the reasons I love this game. There are so many. But I'll tell you one aspect of baseball that is so awesome and so unique. It's the game inside the game. If I can walk people through the game-calling and cat-and-mouse between the catcher. That's what I miss so much. I feel like managing gives me some of that. I know this guy sits on the slider so I'm going to give him a sinker and get a ground-ball double play. I'm walking this guy to get to a better matchup with the guy on-deck because I know we have the bases loaded but this guy is definitely hitting it on the ground and we'll have a chance to turn the double play and get out of it.

And then there is the roar of expectations from the crowd, and that feeling you get from your pitcher when he pumps his fist coming off the field, having punched guys out to get out of a jam. The place is going nuts and you're left trying to slow down your heart rate while the fans are on their feet.

The attention and focus you have to have at certain moments while playing the game within the game . . . God, I miss that, man. God almighty, that's so much fun. I loved it.

Then there is that ultimate feeling. That moment you win a championship, like I did with the Red Sox in 2013 and the Cubs in 2016.

It's hard to explain. It really is. It's greater than anything that happens as a family. Marriage? Childbirth? You're happy but it's not like this in the sense it's a group of people who come together, and it's this moment. It's twenty-five or thirty people who are all putting the puzzle together, constantly attacking, trying to win, and combating all the negative stuff that can happen. And you're in it all together. And you're part of it. You're able to do that, and do it with guys next to you who all have the same goal and mentality of, "We're going to do this! We've got this! We're ready for anything!" You're going to do this, we got this. Are you going to try this? Nope, we're going to do that. We're the best in the world and we're going to prove it. It's fucking awesome, man. There are people that will tell stories about it, and live it, and you can high-five them when talking about it.

I will never forget one of my favorite moments when Stephen Drew hit a home run in Game 6 of the 2013 World Series and I was on-deck and something just clicked in my brain when he hit it. I knew it was gone so I immediately turned around and watched the fans. That's the greatest thing you can do as an athlete. Our success is really cool, but to see all the fans rise up together, high-fiving and watching strangers hug. Shit, I get chills just thinking about it.

I remember all the emotions that came when I caught that last out in 2013. I thanked the umpire, the good Lord, and then ran to our pitcher, Koji Uehara, and lifted him into the air. I never felt a lighter man in my life. And then after we're partying at Game On, the bar in the back of Fenway, and Dustin Pedroia comes over to me and says, "Rossy, how does it feel?"

I was like: "I don't really know. I don't know how it feels."

He goes, "You won't. It's going to be a long time." You have to come to realize so much, including how many things have to go right.

There are so many perfect moments like that. But I get it, this isn't a perfect game, either.

The pace of the game, for instance, can be better, no doubt. I want pressure and I want action. I like the feeling of a fast break in basketball, and while baseball isn't really built for that kind of thing, we can have more urgency. And when there is, the athleticism of our game will shine through. I believe that. There are so many of them, whether it's infielders making great plays or outfielders running down balls. You should be captivated by the game. I know I am more than not. I find myself clapping more as a manager than I did as a player. A guy makes a great catch and my arm goes up. You don't find a lot of managers that do that, but I do. I can't help myself because I'm a fan, and those are the moments built for our fandom. Make a catch? Hell, yeah! Let's go score some runs. By making it all a little faster paced, I think we can appreciate all those moments a little more.

But no matter what, I appreciate it all. How can you not?

Alex Cora, Manager

Alex just gets it. And when you're a player in the major leagues, that's what you yearn for, a manager who not only puts his guys in the best position to succeed, but understands what they're all about. When I played for Alex in Boston, that skill set was put on display every single day, which was a big reason we won those 108 games in 2018 and celebrated that World Series championship. He has gone from college superstar to hot prospect to major league utilityman to ESPN analyst to big-league bench coach to world champion manager.

In my mind, the biggest challenge managing in this day and age of Major League Baseball doesn't actually have to do with the game.

All of a sudden you're the face of the franchise. It's not like I'm the star player or something like that, but you're the spokesman and that's very hard to do. It's like that more than it has been. You talk multiple times before the game and then after the game. That's at least twice a day starting way back in spring training. And you know what? You better be consistent. For me, that whole process is the biggest challenge when it comes to modern-day managing. And when I took the job, I had no idea.

I went from zero to this because when I was in Houston, none of the coaches were allowed to talk to the media. And when I was a player, I had no idea about the manager's responsibilities, which really weren't what they are now. But every little thing is out there, and there is this constant thirst for information and content and the manager is the one expected to deliver it all more than anybody.

You also want to know what is being said without getting consumed with what is being said. That's not easy, either. I know how it works, having worked in the media with ESPN, so I can listen and read and understand what they're trying to do without it bothering me. The manager has to not only have the pulse of the team, but also better be able to gauge the rhythms surrounding that clubhouse.

It's good to give your coaches their voices, and let them put themselves out there, but it can be tricky. The message has to remain the same. Then there is building the reputation of being able to feed the media without saying too much. Let's be real, nobody wants to be boring. There's a fine line, especially with everything going on in society these days. Sometimes as the manager you have to talk about stuff that has very little to do with baseball that you really have no desire to talk about. But, once again, it's the job. Now something happens in the world and you have to do your research and see what's really going on before you say something stupid. It's not sports, but it's always managing.

And know this: Managing 162 games—and hopefully then some—is hard. That's a lot of games and a lot of days. You really have to balance winning and protecting your players, health-wise. Now, you are constantly getting updates from the medical team gauging the status of each player's health. It helps, but it only adds to the challenge to get twenty-seven outs with whatever personnel you have available. This isn't how it used to be, I guarantee that.

When I first came up, if a pitcher was on a roll, the manager wasn't usually going to take his foot off the gas. That guy was pitching until he cooled off. There were no color-coded cards measuring availability like I get on my desk every single day. That old way, it doesn't work anymore.

Honestly, while the increased scrutiny when it comes to players' availability might make managing tougher, it's probably for the better. There is a lot of stuff in our game like that—positive steps in the right direction. But I'll tell you what hasn't been for the better: the time television is adding to these games.

Everyone talks about speeding up the game, but there are so many times we are just waiting, and waiting, and waiting for TV. And I get it. There is a business side of it. But can't we just do it like soccer and put the advertising in while we're playing? So you can complain about the players and their pace, but let's start looking at the television stuff. Let's learn from the World Cup!

Adam Wainwright, All-Star Pitcher

Adam has always been the guy who got it. By the time I joined the Cardinals in 2012, he had already been in the big leagues for seven seasons. He paved the way for literally two generations of players in that St. Louis clubhouse, still going strong after seventeen years in the big leagues. He just gets it. Always has. When Adam pitches, people stop to watch. When Adam talks, people stop to listen. Adam Wainwright is the epitome of everything you want as a teammate, ballplayer, and mentor.

Times have changed. For instance, rookie hazing and that kind of stuff has gotten dramatically different. There's much less of it. But as far as being a good teammate, I mean, I think it's just about lifting the guys up, always finding the best in them, and then challenging them when maybe they're not living up to what the standards are or what you think they can do. I think that's the best way to approach things. But I think the key to it all is being able to speak into people's lives and being authentic with them all the time. Just always rooting for them and loving on them. When you are about them constantly, and they know it, then it gives you a right to speak into their life when it gets tough sometimes.

When I came up, I was surrounded by super-professional guys. Chris Carpenter was amazing to me. He taught me a lot about pitching and taught me a lot about how to be a professional. Guys like Jason Marquis. Guys like Braden Looper. They spent every day with me when I was a rookie. Those two guys really spoke into my life, which meant so much because they had been in the game for so long. It wasn't only that. They had an approach on how to do it. Grab a bag of beers. Grab some water. Make sure you do this, this, and this. Make sure you're here on time. Make sure you wear this, this, and this. There are a lot of guys that really taught me a lot about baseball, but those were the main guys.

In St. Louis, it's always been about promoting guys to take up for the next guy, which is a good thing. Good leaders exist to replace themselves. So what we're trying to do is train everybody in here to be professionals and to be winners, passing on the great current legacy that was passed on to us. That's how it's been since I've been here, and hopefully it continues after I'm gone.

Just because there's not a "C" on the jersey doesn't mean there are no captains in the clubhouse. I think there are always two or three guys in that class, guys who easily wear it. You know, the guys that when they stand up and talk people listen and congregate to. Guys everybody knows have earned the right to speak into people. I can't speak to other sports, but that's how it is here, and it works.

I do think baseball is on the right path. Baseball is still a great game. There are always going to be people who don't like baseball, and there are always going to be people who love it. The game of baseball is great. I do think baseball could do a better job of having fans get access to players to show that baseball is not boring. Baseball is fun. We have to show the personalities, get out there and meet people. Bring the game to them. I think that would be a neat thing. I think we're getting there, which is important because this is such a great game.

Kurt Busch, NASCAR Driver

Kurt is one of the best drivers ever to get behind the wheel of a car in the history of NASCAR. But, just as important, he is yet another high-profile athlete from a completely different sport that has been driven by baseball, learning all of its lessons and using them as fuel for his own career.

Man, when I got to sing "Take Me Out to the Ballgame" at Wrigley Field, that was everything. I felt like I was twelve years old all over again. Living the life of a Cubs fan, watching over my fellow fans. And to top it off, my high school baseball coach was one of those singing along in the stands. It was a dream.

That feeling baseball gives me has never gone away.

When I was a kid, my mom always bought me baseball gloves and baseball bats, always telling me I should really try that sport instead of racing. My dad was a racer at the local track, so he was pushing that. But baseball was never far behind, with my uncle taking me to the Las Vegas Triple-A team all the time just to keep my interest going, with my mom whispering that baseball should be my path all the while. "It's safer than racing," she would say.

I stuck with racing, but baseball was always there, with the Cubbies always on WGN. I loved the Cubs. Ryne Sandberg. He was the best. He was my guy.

One of the things I always loved about baseball was the team sports side of it. Looking back, that was always really important. Growing up, I was always the shortstop or catcher and just wanted to do whatever I could to make the team better. I also loved being the leadoff guy. Just put the bat on the ball and go run. That was my thing. But then I got to high school and kids were starting to get bigger than me and I wasn't growing as fast as them, and my dad saw that. Hence, the racing career.

But there are so many parallels I can draw from baseball to what I'm doing now, or even like someone in a band. In a sense, we're a group and I'm the lead singer. I'm the pitcher. The guy in the middle of it all. And you have to have the team leader while all the other guys are doing their thing. You can't make the music on your own, whether it's in music, racing, or baseball.

Another cool thing about racing and baseball is how you can really pick it apart, talk about it, and that only gets you more into it. Once you jump into it, that allows you to understand it on another level. I love that about baseball. Sure, you can have your moments where things get dull in any sport, but it's always a matter of simply respecting what it takes to win. Once you understand all those ins and outs, that's where you really fall in love with the sport.

And I'll tell you what, when I come to a ballpark it's the same as going to the racetrack. You just have to see it. You have to smell it. You have to feel it. That's such a great feeling. I get that feeling so many times at the track, and I really got that feeling when I got to go to Game 5 of the 2016 World Series. That's just so electric.

Then there was that moment the Cubs actually won. I was just sitting at home back in Charlotte soaking in Game 7, thinking about all the people who got this chance to experience the feeling of that night. My grandmother was born in 1929 and she never had, and then they finally did. The emotion was like winning the biggest race and then some. It was spiritual, for sure.

I'm a Cubs fan and always will be. I just hope people in this era jump into baseball like I did, because it's worth it.

Gar Ryness, Batting Stance Guy

Gar hits a sweet spot for all those baseball fans who grew up not only play-ing, but also idolizing and imitating. Some time ago, he discovered his abil-ity to mirror any batting stance that has ever been put on display in the major leagues. He likes to say it's the "least marketable skill" in the United States, but it is a talent that has earned him fans, including David Letterman and legions of major leaguers. When it comes to defining what kind of fun base-ball can supply, "Batting Stance Guy" is a good place to start.

My name is Gar Ryness and I love baseball. I love my wife and children more, but they haven't been around as long as baseball, so there's a good chance that my memory of Sid Bream's slide in the 1992 National League Championship Series and Dan Gladden's 1987 mullet are more vivid than the two things my wife just told me to remember at the grocery store.

But I never really understood the gravity of my love for the game until I started deconstructing my fan origins while writing a book. In first grade I repeatedly got in trouble with the teacher during coloring time, because I was ruining all the green crayons. Each day I simply chose to draw a baseball field, leaving my classmates without any green to highlight their non-baseball-related drawings. Every penny I earned from my paper route was spent on baseball cards. My second-grade Halloween costume was Pete Rose. My third-grade costume was Gary Carter. It's only now when I say these things aloud that it sounds strange. What Northern California kid went as a Montreal Expos catcher for Halloween? Ever?

We had a rule in our house. My brother, sisters, and I were only allowed to watch seven hours of TV a week. *This Week in Baseball* and NBC's *Game of the Week* took up the bulk of that time, with *The Cosby Show* (can I still say that?) and *Family Ties* taking the rest. When the TV was off, I'd take a random set of twenty-five baseball cards, go to the living room, draft a lineup, and fictitiously reenact an entire game with a Wiffle bat, glove, and my imagination. Daryl Boston would lead off in left field, Ken Landreaux in center field, Greg Walker at first base, Mike Schmidt at third base, Ken

Singleton in right field, Dave Engle at catcher, Dickie Thon at shortstop, Jerry Royster at second base, then the pitcher. That lineup is insane, no rhyme or reason, not all American League or National League, not heavy with players from a particular team, not a bunch of All-Stars. In fact, you might never have heard of some of them. Oh, here comes Al Cowens to pinch-hit for Jerry Augustine.

When I was twelve, the most important thing in my life was taken away from me. I was a starting pitcher for our Little League All-Star team for ten- and eleven-year-olds. It was a league that twice had teams play in Williamsport for the Little League World Series, so there seemed a chance that I had a future with limitless possibilities. Right around my twelfth birthday, I felt a tremendous pain in my right shoulder. Ten months of tests revealed that I had a rare bone tumor the size of a golf ball in my right humerus— something that is not humorous at all.

I was crushed to miss a quarter of seventh grade and have my right arm in a sling while on a crutch. They took bone out of my back to place in the shoulder where the tumor had eaten away the bone, so walking was difficult. The only bright side to the surgery was that my parents got my favorite player, Kent Hrbek, to wish me well with a letter that I should probably get framed someday. Most days some combo of Andy Gustafson, Kevin McCready, Mike Russello, and Todd Harlow would play stickball in my front yard. Not wanting to sit out, I began to pitch left-handed while my normal throwing right arm was in a sling. Senior League (thirteen- to fifteen-year-olds) tryouts came two months after the surgery, and the doctors said it would be impossible for me to play right-handed. I didn't hesitate in my decision to play the entire season left-handed.

Parents and coaches found my story heartwarming and courageous and fully supported my decision. Sadly, the ball didn't cooperate, lacking the courage to go where I aimed it. Though they were supportive, I'm also not sure my teammates found being on the receiving end of my throws very heartwarming. I got through the season but, in the cold, harsh reality of Little League, it wasn't very pretty. I wasn't exactly Jim Abbott.

My right arm healed enough for me to play the following year as a righty. I made the team all four years of high school as the last guy on the bench. Occasionally getting into a game, I was mostly there for comic relief and emotional support for a group of players who were much better than I was ever going to be.

When I went away to college, my baseball career ended, but, as a resident of Northern California attending Syracuse University, I started to take some cross-country road trips. Andy McHargue, a classmate from Oakland and a fellow baseball fan, joined me for these adventures. On those trips we saw nineteen baseball games. I didn't know it at the time, but this was the beginning of my journey to see a game in every stadium. After accomplishing that bucket list, my oldest daughter only has games at Marlins, Rays, Tigers, Pirates, and Reds stadiums remaining.

No longer buying baseball cards or needing autographs, I began to interact with females and see the world. I learned quickly that wearing a Kent Hrbek jersey to college parties wasn't the best way to impress the ladies.

College was a blur of intramural softball, cold winters, and occasional class attendance. I think it's safe to say that anyone who knew me in college will be surprised to find out that I've become a published author.

Through all of these experiences, I've never stopped imitating baseball players' batting stances. It's generally been a silly party trick or just a way to enhance a Wiffle Ball game, but it's something I've never been able to shake. It's like riding a bike. With that said, as I've started thinking about all the details of my life, I've started to feel like Chazz Palminteri turning around in *The Usual Suspects* after Roger "Verbal" Kint has told him the incredible tale. Chazz sees all the evidence on the wall after Kint is gone and is stunned. It's strange to wake up one day in my late forties, married, with two daughters, working a normal job, balding, athletically past my prime, and realize that I am a completely insane baseball fan. It may sound crazy, but I really never knew until it was all laid out in front of me.

Recently, I took a friend to a MLB baseball game for his first time. We watched Shohei Ohtani pitch and hit and I tried to explain how every day at the park you may see something for the first time. But what he's doing no one has seen in a hundred-plus years. I wanted my friend to take a deeper look at the game I—and, most likely, you—love. Baseball, if nothing else, is a game full of details. Its wonderfully slow pace allows for the subtleties and nuances of its characteristics and moments to be magnified for everyone to see. But as with most things in life, we all need to be reminded occasionally where to look.

There are a lot of things to love about baseball, but it's the phenomenon of the stance that caught my attention. It's the celebration of the individual in a team sport, a quick show of personality and flash in a world that generally looks for conformity. It's about music and theater and jazz hands and obsession and consistency (or inconsistency). Other sports have quirky actions that players perform when all eyes are on them—free throws, putting routines, end zone dances, high sticking, soccer players feigning injury—but nothing matches what hitters in baseball do at the plate.

As humans, we often brush off what we see in front of us. We sometimes forget to really absorb what's going on around us. I have absorbed baseball and its cavalcade of personalities and I love it.

There are thousands of players I could tell you about. But the ten batting stances that made me fall in deep love with baseball are: (10) Rod Carew, (9) Phil Plantier, (8) Cal Ripken Jr., (7) Mickey Tettleton, (6) Gary Sheffield, (5) Rickey Henderson, (4) Julio Franco, (3) Tony Batista, (2) Craig Counsell, (1) Kevin Youkilis.

The best thing about baseball is that almost every hitter has his moment. Whether it's the flip of the bat and a rookie's excited run to first on a walk-off homer or the over-the-top reaction of a utility player to a brushback pitch, there are moments of individual absurdity that happen every day in baseball.

Dylan Cease, Pitcher

One of the great things about joining the White Sox is getting a chance to see Dylan pitch. He is truly one of the best young starters in the game, and has an elite mustache, to boot. He is a great example of a kid who was ultra-talented from the first time he picked up a baseball but was forced to learn how to power through the pitfalls of the game to reach the mountaintop. Baseball never makes it easy, but as Dylan has shown us, fighting through the tough times in this game offers the best kind of lessons.

Everyone's story of falling in love with baseball is different. The best I remember, mine started when I was about five years old with my dad hitting me ground balls. We had this asphalt driveway, and I just remembered him smoking cigars, hitting away. I always will remember the smell of those cigars and taking the time to field those grounders. Puffing away. Practicing all the time.

I just loved practice. Loved it. I would want to go hit batting practice for two more hours until my dad would finally drag me off the field.

And if I wasn't playing I was watching the Braves, rooting for Chipper Jones and those guys. I was just obsessed with it. It didn't hurt that I was naturally good at it, too, so I always had that desire to go out and throw or catch. Me and my twin brother, Alec, would go out there and one of us would sit on a bucket and be the catcher while the other pitched. It was nonstop.

I would also cut out pictures and stats off the internet, printing up guys like Chipper and Manny Ramirez and all the best players and making sort of homemade baseball cards.

I was so into it, but I understand why some kids aren't. If you're not naturally gifted at it, it's not going to be as fun, sitting there and failing over and over again. I could go out and smash the ball all over the place, so for me it was fun. If you don't have that ability it can be tough. Failing in baseball can be right in your face more than any other sport.

You don't want to be embarrassed. You have to get over that, and it isn't always easy for some kids.

I was fortunate that I was talented. It was a reality that started hitting home when my dad would tell me people would come up to him at tournaments and say this or that about "the twins." I knew I was one of the better players from the get-go, but still a lot of it doesn't hit home until you hear just the right thing from just the right person. For example, just recently, White Sox closer Liam Hendricks told me I was one of the most talented starting pitchers he had seen. That was something.

I think those compliments as you get later in your career can mean even more because there have been more obstacles you've overcome at that point. It's hard to establish yourself at this level to the point where you're recognized as a good player. You have to have sustained success for a decent period of time, which, believe me, isn't easy to do. Those compliments stick. Yeah, I was better than the other kids, but that doesn't mean I didn't have to overcome a lot to get the kind of pat on the back Liam offered.

There is so much powering through when it comes to a baseball career, and baseball, in general. There's nothing but powering through. The minor leagues are miserable, and even when you get to the majors it's not like it's some insane cakewalk.

For me, two things stick out when it comes to reflecting on roadblocks. My senior year of high school, I was supposed to be a first-rounder and I tore my UCL in my pitching elbow, so for the first two years of professional baseball with the Cubs I had to rehab. It was my first time away from home and I was just uncertain as a whole that I would be the same pitcher. I didn't even really know what I was doing. You have all eyes on just cruising through that senior year of high school and then all that happens. It was a little overwhelming. The other obstacle came when I finally got to the big leagues in 2019 and I struggled. Those first two seasons were challenging, to say the least.

Sometimes you just need someone to give you the right direction. For me that was White Sox pitching coach Ethan Katz, when he said, "Hey, I have a way to fix that." And, sure enough, he did, and it felt like in an instant. Just working on pitching differently with the lower half of my body. That was it. I have been able to build on that and it's been completely different. It's funny how that works sometimes.

Since then I have felt like the same baseball player I was before, in so many ways. I can be myself just knowing that I'm here to do a job and that's the most important thing. I think people have recognized that. As long as I'm treated with respect and kindness, that's all anybody can ask for.

I can't complain. Baseball has been really good to me, starting with those cigar-smoke-filled ground ball sessions in that Georgia driveway.

David Price, All-Star Pitcher

David has become one of my best friends in baseball, and, you know what? He's really smart. I love talking about the state of baseball with him, whether it was as his teammate with the Red Sox or Dodgers, or now through phone calls and text messages from three time zones away. It's great talking about all that is right, all that is wrong, and all that he has learned since first coming into the major leagues in 2008 after being taken with the first overall pick in 2007 just the year before. He cares about the game, every little bit of it.

Jewelry. It's changed a lot. Now, you see a lot of guys wearing earrings and whatever but when I first got into baseball that was a reward for making the All-Star team. Now it's normal. Every day.

It started probably right around when they started Players' Weekend. They suddenly started letting us have fun. Nicknames. Jewelry. Wear what you want. Finally, everything started moving in the right direction. Before, the only guys who were allowed to wear anything were the established guys, Barry Bonds or Ken Griffey Jr. If you were a young player, it would be absolutely frowned upon.

It wasn't like you just decide to go out there with a bunch of jewelry on. It just didn't happen.

But then guys started doing it more and more. They started being themselves on the field, not worrying about what others thought. That was the great thing about playing for Joe Maddon. He just always said in spring training: "Be yourself. I don't care what you wear. I don't care how you dress. Just be comfortable." He just wanted you to be comfortable in your own skin, and I think that's good. All we want are guys to be themselves.

There's a way to go, but it's definitely getting better. [Commissioner] Rob Manfred is trying to have a relationship with the players and I think that is going to help. At least now he's listening to what players have to say and asking players what they think. He's finally hearing from us and trying to repair the relationship.

The shoe and glove things were perfect examples.

Before, they would only let us wear cleats with two colors on them, and they had to be approved. And every glove couldn't have colors on it. Now it has loosened up, and it should. They needed to understand that the shoes are one of the first things kids are looking at and trying to emulate. Baseball finally understanding that it's important for players to be able to express themselves through different kinds of cleats was something that helped gain the trust of the players. I wore blue laces the other day. A few years ago, believe or not, that would have never happened.

I remember seeing Eduardo Escobar of the Mets and seeing him wear some sick cleats that had nothing to do with the Mets' colors. I thought they were so cool. And you know what? I bet there were a lot of kids watching his game that were drawn in because of those cleats. Not every pitch or play in baseball is going to be exciting. That's just the reality. So we have to find other stuff that attracts the younger generations.

The other part of it is the players—no matter how much time they have in the game—feel like they can wear what they want, when they want. It has to start with the kids who are coming up, even in the minor leagues. I remember being back in Triple-A and you were always watching what you wore and what you did because there were a lot of guys who had been in the big leagues and got sent back down, so they were keeping the same strict rules they felt had to be kept in check. A lot of times they were pretty salty and didn't make it all that fun to be around. That had to change, and I think it has.

Now, the kids in the minors—especially the young studs who are coming up—are almost treated like they're in the big leagues. You are allowed to have your own thing, and I think that carries over when they get to the majors. They are their own people. They have their own approach to the game. And everyone can see it.

The game has definitely changed a lot, and hopefully the younger fans have taken notice.

Matt Strahm, Pitcher

One look at Matt and you know he is his own man, living the life of the individualistic major leaguer that MLB should be asking for more of. As of 2022, he was one of just twenty big leaguers in the history of the game who hailed from North Dakota. But Matt has started to stand out in so many more ways than just his home state roots. The animated lefty has continued to make his mark on the mound—with some of the longest hair in the bigs flailing about with each pitch. He has also prioritized the fun off the field, running a YouTube show about baseball cards. And, best of all, Matt is not afraid to say exactly what he thinks when it comes to this game he clearly loves.

Shoes. Hair. Personality. All of it matters to the kids who are trying to fall in love with the game. What's the big deal if we're wearing neon pink cleats, or neon green, if it matches your personality and that's who you are? It's not like we have middle fingers painted on our cleats or anything like that. I guess we have rules, but I don't look at them. I just do whatever I'm going to do with my cleats. If someone tells me something different I'll switch them, but you aren't going to change once you've started.

I never thought I was hurting anybody by painting my cleats. I get it that it used to be where you were only allowed a certain amount of colors, but that seemed silly.

Now, I have a cleat guy. I met him through Mike Clevinger and my agent. The first ones he did were in 2018 when he made them *Sandlot* themed, from the movie. He painted all the characters, the dog, everything. He has done such a great job. He also made some for me to wear that had all five of the big leaguers out of North Dakota—including myself—and then the back was a North Dakota license plate. He did another pair that were Navy themed for when I was in San Diego. Those had a fighter jet on them with an aircraft carrier. Those were really cool. But most of the time it's just color switches and things like that. For me, it's a big deal.

But baseball still hasn't figured it out. When someone makes a great play, you have to work to find it with all the restrictions. Steph Curry does something—like making an insane three-point shot—it's all over the place in like ten seconds. The other day I was reading that Manny Machado sprained his ankle. I couldn't find it anywhere. Making something like that so difficult, how is that growing the game? It should be word vomit everywhere talking about it. Videos. Conversation. You name it. Instead, I'm trying to find the Padres page on my MLB app. People aren't getting newspapers thrown against their door anymore. In fact, what's a newspaper?

It's on the field. It's off the field. It's everything. Baseball just needs to be better.

The marketing of baseball needs to be accessible to everyone. Everyone! That's how you will grow the game. But when it feels like the thirty clubs are keeping it all to themselves, that's not going to grow anything.

We just have to be ourselves and then show everyone that we are the guys who aren't afraid to be ourselves.

I for sure didn't grow my hair out to be part of an image. It just happened and I started to enjoy it. It is what it is, but what it isn't, is some sort of master plan to make people like me. That said, I should be standing out. So should each and every player in their own unique way. But instead the guys getting imitated by the kids are the basketball players, and even the football players who you can't even see when they're playing their game because of the helmets. Baseball has to start doing a better job of getting every little intricacy of our game out there, dispersing it in whatever way possible to the next wave of baseball fans.

In the meantime, I'll keep trying to do my part.

Andy Cohen, Television Personality

Anybody who watches television on a regular basis knows Andy and what he has helped build at the Bravo Television Network. But I know him as one of the thousands of die-hard Cardinals fans I came to appreciate during my time in St. Louis. It's always great to see someone who has become so successful in a high-profile industry like the entertainment world still gravitate to our world of baseball. And when you talk to Andy about the sport, there is no room for interpretation. When it comes to this game, he is ready to spread the good word.

When you grow up in St. Louis, you're a Cardinals fan. That's how it starts. Then you get season tickets and it just goes from there. At least that's my story.

Now, I don't remember my absolute very first memory. I just remember that the ballpark felt like a place where things were going. There were the Clydesdales. There was all the food. There were all the people. And then came the 1982

World Series, when the Cardinals beat the Brewers, and I was hooked. "Celebration" was the theme song and it just all seemed so cool. Ozzie Smith. Willie McGee. They had those powder-blue uniforms. It all just felt like home, like a community along with all the civic pride wrapped up into it. It sounds corny, but having that song, it did all feel like there was something to celebrate. It was a reason to feel good about where you were from and just life, in general.

That's the thing about baseball. It's all very life-affirming and positive. It's just beautiful, and so American. There is just no feeling like when you have a team and they're doing well. There's a romance about it.

When the Cardinals won in 2011, I can still feel that. When David Freese hit that walk-off home run in Game 6, I just cried so much that night. Tears of joy. I remember I was hosting an event and my mom and others were texting me updates, and I was watching clips on Twitter trying to follow along. And then that happened. It was just all so stunning. I ended up going home and rewatching clips all night on ESPN, just bawling my eyes out. I couldn't figure out why I was so emotional, but it was just so exciting. Then when Game 7 came around, I was watching with these friends of mine and just crying through the whole game.

They were like, "Why are you crying?"

I'm like, "You have to understand what this team has been through this whole year and how unlikely this whole scenario is . . . And David Freese is from St. Louis!"

It just meant so much to everyone and made your heart swell. That's what baseball can do.

I look at following baseball like following the Grateful Dead. I'm a big Deadhead. People are just brought up with it and then they go on to share it. You go to a Dead show and the demographic is of all ages. Baseball can grab a hold of you like that because people are brought up playing it. A cynic might say it's too slow for people these days. But when you're brought up on something, like most people are with baseball—both playing and watching—there is going to be some sort of connection. This country might be going to hell, but I do believe, no matter what, baseball will endure. It has to. It means too much.

And listen, this is coming from someone who was horrible in Little League. I remember my last game. I lost it for us. I got up with men on base, we were losing, and had I done something I could have been the hero. But that wasn't how life was working out for me at that point and I struck out. I still remember after the game all the parents took the kids to Dairy Queen, with a parent of one of my friends driving me because I wouldn't let my parents come to the game. My dad wanted to coach but I wouldn't let him because I was so bad. I was embarrassed. On the way to get that ice cream, the mother who was in the front seat said—and I remember this like it was yesterday—"Wow, you lost the game." I came home and I so desperately didn't want to start crying, but once my mother asked me how it went I just broke down. She gave me a big hug.

But the amazing thing was that I still loved baseball.

The next time I wore a baseball uniform was in a celebrity softball game at an All-Star Game. There I was in the locker room and right next to me was Cardinals legend Ozzie Smith. Oh my God! I was so intimidated. All of a sudden, I had this weird feeling I hadn't had since Little League. I was playing the game again and wearing the uniform again. And this time they had the whole uniform, everything including giving us special underwear. I turned to Ozzie and said, "Do we have to wear all of this? Do I have to wear this underwear?" He was like, "No, you can wear your own." I felt like I was four years old all over again and I also felt so protected. I just loved the trappings of it all. I wanted to be in the uniform. I wanted to schmooze with the players. It was such a great exercise for me, taking me so far out of my comfort zone and connecting me to something I love. It was a long way from that ride to Dairy Queen.

I understand that baseball isn't for everyone. There is an element where you either get it or you don't. But so many times something just clicks when you're watching a game that makes it so exciting. That's the beauty of the game. I see it, and so do a lot of my friends.

Jerry Seinfeld took me to a big Mets and Cardinals playoff game. He's a huge Mets fan. We were driving over to the game and he turned and said, "You know, one of us is really going to leave this game upset." So, we agreed in the car right then and there we weren't going to speak of the game at all on the way home. Fortunately, the Cardinals won. Needless to say, it was an awkward drive home because Jerry is like *Mr. Met*. There are plenty of experiences like that because we're all so passionate about the game and our teams. That's just how it is. You want to know how passionate I am about the Cardinals? I named my dog after one of their former pitchers, Michael Wacha. The Cardinals and Dodgers were in the playoffs and Wacha was really doing well as a rookie. I was walking through the stands and everyone was just cheering for this guy. I'm like, "That's it! Wacha!" My dog had a new name, thanks to baseball.

The game just means so much in so many ways. I know. I'm reminded of it almost every day.

. . .

And there's more . . .

Jon Hamm, Actor

I remember two things about falling in love with baseball. First, I can remember my first trip to Busch Stadium. It was like the opening scene in *Bull Durham* where the camera comes through and all of a sudden you see the field and—even though there wasn't a stitch of real grass because of the artificial turf in the seventies—I just remembered it all being so green and breathtaking. This wasn't like it was represented on TV. Being there was just so different. And then five or six years later, I got to go to my first World Series game. Those are the kind of indelible memories that made the game stick for me. I love it. The absolute greatest thing about baseball is that it's the only sport where there is no time limit. It can go on forever, and I usually find myself hoping it does.

Nestor Cortes, All-Star Pitcher

I fell in love with baseball at about four years old when coaches started lobbing it into me. But what really made baseball take off for me was five years later when the Marlins won their championship in 2003. I had become a huge Marlins fan, and when that happened, my ambition to play the game skyrocketed. The game is incredible. It can be slow at times, but when you come to appreciate every little thing about it and what everybody does, day in and day out, it really is incredible. Now, to see what everyone has to do to get ready and prove you belong, and how much work goes into it, that makes you appreciate it even more. There is no other sport where you have to fight through failure and the tough times. But when you come out on the other side, and you're able to achieve your dreams, that's when it really hits home how special this game is.

Julio Rodriguez, All-Star Outfielder

I fell in love with baseball just going out on the streets as a kid, every day, with my friends. We would play five or six hours, as long as we could, after school, before school. It was just about having fun with my friends and appreciating those moments. Baseball was the only sport that could do that for me.

J. D. Martinez, All-Star Designated Hitter

What I love about baseball is how you don't have to be a certain size or have an unbelievable level of skill. It's a mental sport as much as anything. You can have guys like Aaron Judge and be born with amazing genes, or not, and still make an impact on the game. There are just such a wide variety of athletes who play this game and can excel in their own ways. No other sport is like that. I realized that early on, but for me it really hit home when I would go over to our family friend Paul Casanova's house. He had played ten years in the big leagues and he would just tell me stories of all the great players and what they did. It started hitting home for me. I remember saying, "I want to be able to tell stories like this one day." I was just eating it up. And that's what is great about baseball, passing on every little thing that makes the whole experience great. Those stories meant everything to me. So has baseball.

Travis d'Arnaud, All-Star Catcher

There are so many different things that can happen in a baseball game, and you see something new every single day, more so than in any other sport. And, really, it's more of a game of chess than anything, which I love. The cat-and-mouse game, I love it all. I love being around a group of friends who are like brothers, joking all day and then going out and playing games. I love how hard it is to hit a baseball. I love how difficult it is to command a baseball when throwing it. But we also have to realize that all these little things aren't being taught to fans, and it's being forgotten because of it. These are the things that need to be put out there again, how it is a game of chess and makes you think instead of just obsessing over numbers. Kids have to realize that, yeah, it can be really slow but—boom!—there is that moment of passion. All of it is really cool.

Kyle Schwarber, All-Star Designated Hitter

One of the things I have always appreciated is that because we play so many games, if you have a bad day, you know a good one might be right around the corner. You can control that narrative. That's a great thing to experience. It's so different from other sports. It's a team-oriented game where so much is dependent on individual performance. You have to do your job in order for both the guy in front of you in the batting order and the guy behind you to be put in the best position. It's also different because we're the only game where when you are on offense you don't have the ball, and if you fail seven out of ten times you're really freaking good. And, yes, it can be humbling. It's probably more humbling than any other sport. But it's a microcosm of life. The toughest challenges always lead to the most satisfaction. That's what baseball does.

Joe Mantiply, All-Star Pitcher

My favorite part of baseball is something that makes it so unique, getting to meet so many different guys from all over the world and from so many backgrounds. Just getting to share a clubhouse with them and getting to know them. Those are the kinds of memories you end up cherishing forever. I have learned so much in life from just being in the clubhouse and being around different people. It has made me a better person, and, honestly, it's just really, really hard to imagine what my life would be like without this game. I owe everything to baseball.

Corey Seager, All-Star Shortstop

You might start baseball like I did, playing with my older brother and father, but then it goes beyond that. It's a way to get out of the house, start hanging out with friends, and build relationships that last a lifetime. Baseball gives you a family away from your family. There is nothing like it.

Ken Griffey Jr., Hall of Famer

It doesn't matter how big you are, or how small you are, you can play baseball. That's what has always been great about it. There is no eye-test when it comes to a seven-foot guy or a five-foot-five guy. If you can play baseball—hit, run, and throw—you can play. It all comes down to how you deal with failure, because if somebody fails seven out of ten times, they are a Hall of Famer. It's one of those things that if you love it, you are going to stick with it. Did I fall in love with it right away? Yes. My dad playing in the major leagues just made it easier; knowing that there was somebody I could talk to every day who had done it at the highest level made it easier to digest. Before I was even old enough to play, my dad made sure I knew more than half of the rules because he didn't want me making the same mistakes over and over again. He drilled them into me, making sure I was going to learn the game of baseball the right way. There are no left-handed third basemen. There are no left-handed shortstops. There are no left-handed second basemen.

When I was nine years old, I almost quit for three days because I knew all of that. Why? Have you ever heard of a left-handed third baseman? I had a bad coach whose son wanted to play first base because that's where all the action was, so he tried moving me to third. I was like, "All right, I'm going home." I came home and told my parents I was about to quit, and you know what? My dad understood and so did my mom. Having parents who get it is so important. I coached my son for three years in football, and even though I was the offensive coordinator, I never called a play specifically for him. If the head coach wanted him to run the ball, the head coach was going to have him run the ball. Playing Daddy-Ball is not the way to go. Baseball taught me that as a nine-year-old.

Ian Happ, All-Star Outfielder

You fall in love with baseball watching your brother, your father, and your friends. I know I did. It makes you look forward to being around to play the game with all of them. More than any other sport, it's generational. From grandfather, to father, to son. It's just such a beautiful game that teaches you so many life lessons.

Liam Hendricks, All-Star Pitcher

Coming from Australia, what strikes me about baseball is how much diversity there is. You have got thirty teams with guys from all over the world, different hemispheres and different continents. There are guys from all walks of life who are coming to teams in so many different ways. That's the melting pot that is a baseball clubhouse. It's a place where we spend ten hours a day with each other, constantly gleaning all this information of why everyone is so different. It's a great thing.

Ty France, All-Star First Baseman

It's not just baseball, but it's sports in general. They allow you to learn so much by interacting with so many different people and players. Baseball is maybe the best at it. The majority of the reason where I am today is because of baseball. You have to learn so many life lessons and overcome so much. It's something baseball teaches you as a young kid, and because of it life is a little easier. I appreciate that.

Paul Blackburn, All-Star Pitcher

I just remember begging my dad to go outside and hit fly balls to me or play catch. We would do that until the sun went down. It allowed for so many great memories. Baseball is also unique because unlike other sports you kind of need others to play, which allows you to do something with your friends. You build so many relationships. It's tough these days because of attention spans, and we have to figure out ways to entice the younger generation because of it. But what I would say in the meantime is to have patience. When it comes to baseball, it is worth it.

Mookie Betts, All-Star Outfielder

It took me a while to fall in love with baseball. I really didn't enjoy it that much until I got older because I wanted to play basketball. It was the only other sport I could play because my parents wouldn't let me play football. But once I told myself I really wanted to be good at it, that's when I fell in love with it. I think that's the best way to be good at anything, to really dive in and fall in love with it. That's what I did with baseball and I'm glad I did. . . . As I have come to find out, baseball is anything but boring because you have the best skilled athletes playing the hardest game in the world doing all the hardest things you can do. It's an art form.

Paul Goldschmidt, All-Star First Baseman

Baseball is just fun. It's fun to go out there and compete, be with your friends and teammates and simply just run around. But, in the bigger picture, baseball is such a great metaphor for life. You have to deal with failure, and nothing teaches that more than baseball. The game is unfair. You can hit a ball hard or throw a perfect pitch and it still might not go your way. You have to learn how to deal with other people, coaches and teammates. You have to learn how to manage success and not get too excited. Basically, all the things that come with life. Baseball teaches all of those life lessons.

I still remember my first baseball practice, getting out of my mom's minivan and saying, "Mom, I love baseball." That was my first practice. It was in my blood and I always loved it. For me, it's always been a passion. Sure, there is plenty of failure, and who likes failure? But baseball reminds you to embrace it. You have to make a choice. Do I just give up, or do I work? Do I practice? Do I keep going after my goals? We are all going to fail, but it is the choices when it comes to reacting to those failures. Baseball gives you that choice, usually a couple of times a day. As a kid, you might not even realize it. You're just playing and having fun, and then all of a sudden you strike out or make an error. You learn those lessons. I don't want to just single out baseball, but I do because it is my favorite. I mean, you're playing the piano and you have artistic failures that are built into your life. I just love baseball.

Another big part of it is figuring out what you love doing, and parents should also understand that. My parents never forced me to play, and I'm sure they were nervous I would hate it because they loved it so much. They just kept letting me play. And I'm sure glad they did.

Max Fried, All-Star Pitcher

Baseball doesn't give you instant gratification, but there is so much strategy that goes on. More than just home runs or things like that. It's such an interesting game because there is a huge element of it being such a one-on-one dynamic, but you're also integrated into a team. It's such a balance of having the individual responsibility and taking on your role, but also being part of a team setting where everybody is coming together to try and win. It's so unique. And I learned that watching my older brother and going to the field with a bunch of guys, making lifelong friends. Looking back now, a lot of my core memories are just spending time on those Little League fields, whether it was playing Wiffle Ball or the run-down game Pickle or things like that. Just such great memories, all thanks to baseball.

Austin Riley, All-Star Outfielder

You've got a round bat, and you're trying to hit a round ball. To me, it's one of the hardest things to do in sports. It takes so much time working on it, which is why work ethic and hard work is what makes you succeed in baseball. You have to take so much pride in it because it is so difficult. That's what makes this game so unique. For me, it just brought me so much joy, playing in the backyard, simulating all those big moments in the bottom of the ninth. Then those moments become reality and it's such an adrenaline rush. You just can't explain it. For me, it's just something that isn't like other sports.

David Bednar, All-Star Pitcher

I love the competition that comes with baseball, knowing it's just me versus the hitter. That's it. Me against him. It's so much fun, and it always has been. It should be fun. It should be like when you're playing backyard Wiffle Ball, trying to pimp homers and talking crap to your buddies after striking them out. It doesn't have to be a buttoned-up game, and it shouldn't be. Just go out and play.

Shawn Green, Former All-Star Outfielder

Baseball is just such a beautiful experience. It's so different from any other sport. It says something there is no clock because it's supposed to be a leisurely experience, where the spaces between the action are just as important as the action. Between every pitch there is a break. Basketball? There is a constant flow, and the same with football, where you might have a little bit of a break but nothing like baseball. There are all these intervals of space between all the excitement. We have to embrace that excitement. There's plenty of it if you just take the time to look for it.

CC Sabathia, Former All-Star Pitcher

Baseball is such a family-oriented game. I learned how to play the game from my grandfather, who passed it down to my dad. It's just one of those games you keep passing down, and for me to get the opportunity now to pass it down to my boys and let them enjoy the game like I have is special. This is America's Pastime because of that reason, because it is such a family game. Loving the game. Following the teams. It's so deeply rooted in us.

Anthony Volpe, Top Infield Prospect

At this point in time, baseball just has so many exciting athletes that make you remember why the game is so great. It reminds you of the old-time players, the guys who had so much flair. They are all doing stuff that nobody has seen before, which is what baseball is all about. It's why I fell in love with baseball. I remember waiting for my dad to come home from work, making the hour-or-so trip from New Jersey to New York City. He would arrive and we would go down to the park and within thirty minutes we would be playing nine against nine. My parents never forced it on me but they just let me fall in love with it. And now, it's still my passion.

Taj Bradley, Top Pitching Prospect

Going to the field. Going to camps. It was just all fun. It still is. I have that same feeling every time I go to the ballpark. This shouldn't be about trying to get a scholarship as a twelve-year-old or something like that. Just go out to the field and have fun. That's what changed for younger kids, all that pressure. Just go out and love it every day you play. I know I do.

Mike Burrows, Top Pitching Prospect

My dad was just so into baseball and had such a passion for it, which was what allowed me to have those experiences of going to games and seeing the big-league players and all that atmosphere that comes with it. I just remember seeing Jonathan Papelbon run out of the bullpen at Fenway Park and hearing that song, "I'm Shipping Up to Boston," playing with everyone chanting. You get chills from that kind of stuff. It all just resonated for me and I knew that was what I wanted to do. This was where I wanted to be one day. Those players—Pedro Martinez, Josh Beckett—were the guys I wanted to be, the guys I looked up to. I loved watching them. I wanted to be like them. There are plenty of those types of guys playing now. Kids just have to take the time to experience it like I did. Believe me, it's worth it.

Terry Francona, Manager

I think it's your perception. For us, baseball is the greatest sport in the world. People love football. If you love

basketball, good for you. But, for me, I like box scores. I like
the stories that come with baseball. It's not for everybody,
but that doesn't mean we shouldn't think it's the best. I think
we do a poor job of explaining to people how much we do
love baseball. As an industry, we need to do a better job. It's
not instant gratification, which is our society, not just in
sports. If you take a few seconds to understand what is really
going on then you fall in love with it. I love a good pitchout
or a guy stealing. That's me. I will never change. You don't
have to be satisfied instantly, but in our world you have video
games and people skip the commercials. That's where we
are. But baseball is something different. It's great. I love it.

ACKNOWLEDGMENTS

I would like to thank my beautiful wife and English teacher, Ashley. From correcting my grammar when we were nineteen-years-old, to all that you do each and every day throughout our lifelong journey. You are the epitome of perfection.

Thank you to my wonderful kids. Even though you guys are not old enough to read or understand this book, one day you will, and I hope you truly enjoy and appreciate the message. So much of it was for you.

Thank you to my siblings—Lennae, Christopher, Nolan, and Michael. You are the ones who molded me into what I am today.

Mom, thank you for always supporting me and pushing me out of my comfort zone. This book is an example of that. You always told me to challenge myself and keep practicing.

Dad, thank you for showing me what faith, courage, and discipline look like. You are the man I strive to be. I can't thank you enough.

Rick, thank you for being a loving husband and father. Your patience is something I admire and used throughout my writing.

Wendy, thank you for showing me what loyalty looks and feels like. You are the best second mother I could ever wish for.

To my teammates from the Cardinals, Red Sox, Dodgers, and White Sox: You all have played an integral part of my life and baseball career. Without you all this would have never been possible.

My literary agent Susan Canavan, thank you for the countless hours of work and support. You believed in greatness and have supported us from Day 1. We did it!

Keith Wallman, the man who has done so well a million times, along with all the hard-working people at Diversion, thank you for taking the leap of faith and showing the world what two men can achieve thanks to the right focus, passion, and guidance.

Cooper "Coop" Leonard, thank you for being the mastermind behind the curtains. You—along with our other young "Baseball Isn't Boring" star Nate Gardner—have used your creative personalities to build a brand from nothing. Yes, baseball is not boring.

Rob Bradford, my partner in crime, you are one of my dearest friends and the favorite teammate I have ever had. Thank you for trusting me with a partnership we will have for life. You always knew we could do something special (even after I failed to come through with that Cy Young prediction on your radio show all those years ago). I love you like family, Bradfo.

ABOUT THE AUTHORS

JOE KELLY is a ten-year major league veteran, having won the World Series with both the Boston Red Sox and Los Angeles Dodgers. He also went to the World Series with the St. Louis Cardinals, the franchise that selected him in the third round of the 2009 Major League Baseball Draft. He currently plays for the Chicago White Sox. Kelly is a Southern California native who shares three young children with his wife, Ashley.

ROB BRADFORD has covered the Boston Red Sox for more than twenty years, covering Major League Baseball for the *Lowell Sun, Lawrence Eagle-Tribune, Boston Herald,* and WEEI. He has written two books: *Chasing Steinbrenner: Pursuing the Pennant in Boston and Toronto* and *Deep Drive: A Long Journey to Finding the Champion Within,* the bestselling autobiography of World Series MVP Mike Lowell.